THIS Bo

BeLon

DIANA LOWE.

Wafflings of a West Country Man

by

Roy Baker

ISBN: 978-1-312-90033-2

In
Our
Village

2004

To Di.
Hope you enjoy reading this.

Kind regards

Roy Baker. x

JANUARY IN OUR VILLAGE

A happy, Healthy and Peaceful New Year to all.

1st. New Years Day.

Well believe it or not this is my twelfth contribution to this month in our village, and so the year is done. When Bob Coombs asked for someone to write a monthly column on flora and fauna in the village I said I would have a go as there were no other takers, but it would have a 'foodies' view on things as that is one of my main topics of conversation. I have always enjoyed growing, gathering, fishing and 'procuring' game. Living in the past is what my family call it that is foraging, bartering and generally obtaining wild and free food.

5th. TWELFTH NIGHT
(old Christmas eve or the eve of Epiphany).

There is very little to find at this time of year in the wild, but depending on the weather you can still fish for eels, pike or perhaps a perch, all of which are good eating. Of course game is still in season and until next month pheasants, partridge duck etc is still good eating. The odd mushroom can still be found in wooded areas such as the oyster mushroom, some bracket fungus and occasionally blewits. There is little in the vegetable department unless you manage to find wild parsnip or carrot and it will mean a lot of digging for little reward. Fruits and nuts are all gone, so there is not much to report.

> Health to thee good apple tree,
> Whence thou may'st bud and whence thou
> may'st blow,
> And whence thou may'st have apples enow.
> Hats full, caps full,
> Three bushel bags full,
> And my pockets full too.

In the garden we have kales, sprouts, leeks, artichokes (Jerusalem and Chinese) and a few stored vegetables. We have already sown, in heat, onions, early leeks, cabbage, cauliflower and early Brussels sprouts.

In the flower garden, snowdrops are breaking and early specie narcissus and crocus are coming to bud. Witch Hazel is flowering as is the chimonanthus praecox with its beautiful scent, so we are on our way in the New Year.

> Plough Monday The first Monday after
> Epiphany.

Now on these winter days when we come in from the cold, the fire is bright we sit at the table to have our dinner and reflect on the year. I have started my meal with a mushroom soup and I remember picking those mushrooms in the autumn. The main course is a roasted stuffed pheasant (free food), with herbs from the garden also the vegetables, potatoes lifted in July, kale I planted in May, carrots I sowed in April and leeks I planted in June, all washed down with a nice bottle of blackberry wine. To follow blackberry and apple pie. We picked the berries in August.

If I had a cow no doubt there would be home produced cheese as well but we won't be going down that road.

22nd. Saint Vincent

I think you will agree it's a far cry from a burger from McDonald's, but it is my belief that we must buy and use local foods, in season, like we did years ago and to encourage the younger generation to cook "REAL FOOD" or we will lose the knowledge to cook like our forefathers.

25th. Saint Ananias.

For my final recipe I am using

AUNTY MARY DREWS Spicy Bread Pudding.

8oz. Bread (crust removed)
2oz. Melted butter
3oz. Soft brown sugar
1 tbsp. Mixed spice
1 egg beaten
6oz. Fruit

half pint milk
Nutmeg
Grated rind of 1/2 Orange

Method; Heat oven to 180. c. Break up bread
and pour over milk leave to soak for 30. Mins.
Add melted butter, sugar, spice and beaten egg
and mix together, add fruit and orange rind.
Spread evenly in a greased 2 pint cake tin,
sprinkle with nutmeg and cook for 1 1/2 hours.

Enjoy your flora and fauna and do get out there
and try some

FEBRUARY

This month is one of sunshine and crisp dry days, flora starts to awaken and buds on the trees start to swell. They promise to burst into a lovely soft green mantle. As you walk around the Village you can see already that the hazel (corylus), catkins are growing longer. Some brave primroses and violets are giving a taste of what is to come later.

Other plants to enjoy now (in the kitchen that is), are chickweed (stellaria media) which can be eaten raw as salad leaves or cooked in a little boiling water, also cleavers or goosegrass (gallium aparine) which can be picked in winter and cooked like spinach.

Common sorrel (rumex acetosa) can be picked as early as February, cook the leaves as you would spinach or with an onion ,carrot and potato makes a fine soup.

February also sees some of our softbilled birds like Blackbirds, thrushes, hedge accentors etc. pairing up and looking for a site to build their nests, just watch them for awhile, a cock will bring a few bits of dried grass to show the hen what sort of mate he is. She in turn will try an old nest and shuffle around in it, then decide it will not do. Bird song is getting stronger and there is an urgency for unpaired to find a mate.

A warm day in February is a dream of April

In our village as you have likely seen there are a number of mammals running around by day, and some by night: we have rabbits everywhere, badgers in most gardens at sometime, foxes and down on the river, after many years we have otters back which is a good sign. Hedgehogs, squirrels and frogs are still in sleep or a semi torpid state (something I know about, the cold has the same affect on me) but will soon think about waking. Well, next month spring will be here and while rabbits are still in season I will give you my rabbit brawn recipe.

Enjoy your flora and fauna.

MARCH

Comes in like a lion and goes out like a lamb.

Spring is here, new life, birds are nesting and baby rabbits are around {see them on the verges along Silk mills road}. Usually the soft billed birds such as the blackbirds, thrushes, robins, blue tits etc. nest before the finches i.e. Gold, bull, green and linnets and so they are sitting their eggs and towards the end of the month we will see them collecting worms, grubs etc. to feed their offspring. The rooks have usually made an earlier start as in February they were busy building at their nest sites, calling, and making quite a din. The herons which frequent the village garden ponds looking for goldfish aren't so evident at the moment, they to are mating now.

1st. MARCH.
Upon St David's day put oats and barley in the clay.

In the hedgerows buds are almost at bursting point and everything seems to take on a look of renewal. In the kitchen now there could be the start of some tasty wild foods such as Hogweed (Heracleum sphondylium) use the shoots and young leaves, which is compared by many as good as asparagus. The corn salad (Valerianella locusta). Don't dismiss our Dandelion (Teraxacum officinale) as you can make wine from the flowers, salad leaves if you blanch them, and a very passable coffee from the root, which is dried then roasted and then ground or blitzed in a food mill then made in the usual way. Nettles while young make a good nettle soup, nettle beer and a green dye was made to colour camouflage in the second world war.

2nd.MARCH

Before St.Chad.
Every goose lays both good and bad.

 In the garden just now daffodils, crocus, primroses, Lenten roses can all be appreciated as can the purple sprouting broccoli, spring greens and kales which bring us to almost the end of our productive year, but already we are potting up onions that were sown on Boxing day, planting shallots and broad beans. Time to for sowing tomatoes, peppers, chillies and aubergine to keep our vegetable food store going for another year.
 In the fauna department we have enjoyed seeing the rabbits at play and the pheasants coming down onto the road at roly poly and even in our lane between Mountway lane and Mountway Road. I drove behind a cool cock pheasant which eventually decided to stroll into the garden on the corner of Mountway road.
 The badgers have at present (because new fences have been erected) given us a wide birth. He

usually digs a little hole and leaves his calling card.

It is time to for little boys with jam jars to look for tadpoles.

Last month I promised you my rabbit brawn recipe

On Mothering Sunday above all other
Every child should dine with its mother.

Rabbit jointed,
2 pigs trotters,
1 onion stuck with cloves,
1 carrot split,
2 bay leaves,
a sprig of thyme,
approx. 10 black peppercorns,
 a little salt,
1 rasher of smoked bacon (the saltpeter in the bacon gives the brawn a better colour).
1 tablespoon lemon juice or white wine vinegar and some chopped parsley.

METHOD:
Put all ingredients except lemon and parsley into a pan and just cover with water. Bring to a boil and simmer for about 2- 3hrs. .
Let meats cool in the liquid. Remove from pan and take all the meats off the bones.

Meanwhile rapidly boil liquid to reduce to half. Chop the meat, not too small, add parsley and mix.

Pack into small basins, add lemon juice to reduced liquid, check seasoning and pour over meat to cover making sure the liquid goes down between the meat. Prise apart with a fork if necessary.

Let cool until it can go into the fridge overnight to set. Turn out of moulds, slice and serve with salads or a crusty bread and runner bean chutney.

(More about this when runner beans are in season).

Enjoy your flora and fauna.

APRIL

*The first day of April some do say
Is set aside for all fools day
But why the people call it so
Nor I nor they, themselves do know*

SPRING HAS COME WHEN YOU CAN PUT A FOOT ON THREE DAISES.

April is a month when everything looks alive, and new. Birds are very busy feeding young, blue tits are said to hatch their young to coincide with a hatch of caterpillars, and they can be seen feeding from dawn to dusk. Blackbirds also are very busy feeding. Tadpoles are changing gradually into small frogs. In the rivers you can now see brown trout as the waters clear, pointing upstream. I can remember as a boy, General Pyman invited me and a friend into the orchard by Pigsloose Lane and said 'you might catch a trout each but don't overdo it '. We duly marched away with one each, and they tasted great.

ON THE THIRD DAY OF APRIL COME THE CUCKOO AND THE NIGHTINGALE

There are in the hedges at the moment, Primroses, catkins and pussy willows. I remember again as a boy at Easter time many mothers took their children and walked through Cometrowe out to the copse to pick primroses.

16

Just after the war we would take lemonade, Marmite sandwiches and hot cross buns and spend the whole day in the copse tying bunches of primroses on hazel sticks. We carried them home to give to mothers who didn't come with us.

In the wild larder at the moment, food is getting more exciting, there is the Hawthorn (Crataegus monogyna) also known as bread and cheese for the young shoots and buds give a nutty flavour to salads, they are quite delicious on their own (do try some). Hairy bittercress (cardamine hirsute) is a tangy hot leaf ideal with ham. Another, (cardamine pratensis) or lady's smock or cuckooflower, so called because it comes into flower when the cuckoo sings, is a good substitute for watercress. Jack by the hedge (alliaria petiolata), which is a garlic mustard, was once valued in making a sauce for salt fish and locally known as 'sauce alone'.

I have left the best until last, for April is the time when two of the very best mushrooms appear, namely the St. Georges mushroom (Tricholoma gambosum) and the even better Morel (morchella esculenta). The morel, chopped with wild garlic (allium ursinum) or ramsons and a few wood pigeons eggs make the very best omelette. By the way, I found and picked about two pounds of morels once on a shrub bed in French Weir, which was top -dressed with bark mulch. The mushrooms only grew on the bark mulch, which must have come from a wood rich in morels and the spoors settled on the bark. So look now if you have mulched your beds, you never know!

In the garden now we are planting onions and sets, peas, carrots, beet, in fact anything that is not frost tender. Indoors it's time to sow tomatoes for putting out in June also I sow my runner beans in pots on the 16th of this month.

I will leave you with my recipe for hot cross buns.

1lb. strong white flour
6 ozs. dried mixed fruit
1 egg
1 oz. Sugar
1 tspn. Salt
1 tspn. each of nutmeg, mixed spice and cinnamon
1 sachet fast action yeast
9 fluid ozs. tepid water
2 oz. butter or veg. oil.

METHOD: Put all dry ingredients in bowl, add all water and egg and mix to a dough. Take out and knead until elastic.

Put into an oiled poly bag to prove until doubled in size. (Keep warm).

Knock the dough back and knead a little. Roll into about 10 – 12 balls and put on baking tray.

Put to prove again in the warm until risen again. Make a flour and water paste and pipe a cross on top. Place in a pre heated oven 200 c. for approx. 12-15 mins.

 Glaze while hot, with sugar and hot water (tablespoon of each mixed)

Just add cream and jam.

Enjoy your flora and fauna!

MAY

The fair maid who, the first of May,
Goes to the fields at break of day,
And washes in dew from the hawthorn tree,
Will ever after handsome be.

In the wild larder, Charlock (sinapsis arvensis),
leaves are a good standby for spinach, while good
king Henry (Chenopodium bonus-henricus)
shoots and young flowering tops, boiled and
eaten with butter are a treat. Ground elder
(aegopodium podagraria), yes that weed you
don't know what to do with is used as spicy
spinach. Wild strawberry (fragaria vesca), is well
worth picking with a little sugar and cream or
make into jam. (They are sweeter than the garden
strawberry.

The spring has sprung, the grass has ris
I wonder where the birdie is
The bird is on the wing
But that's absurd
The wing is on the bird

Our soft -billed birds at the moment are on their
second brood, & despite putting up nest boxes for
our garden birds, we have had them inspected
inside and out by blue tits and robins but this year
so far they have refused to use them. The
Blackbirds have nested in the spotted laurel next
to our arch and the blackbird considers them to

20

close to his nest and therefore drives them away. I live in hope, perhaps next year. Rabbits abound, the herons pass by almost daily now and I just saw five beautiful Buzzards circling, rising higher and higher until almost out of sight, they certainly seem to be on the increase.

In the garden there is still much to do. Outside sow your runner beans on the tenth of May this allows three weeks to germinate and they will be through by the first of June after the frost, (hopefully). Also the end of the month should be safe to plant out your hanging baskets etc, and tomatoes, celery, peppers, courgettes and hope for a good crop. May is also the best time to sow kales, purple sprouting, Savoy cabbages and sprouts for winter greens. I always sow some basil seed now to correspond with a glut of tomatoes so then we make a tomato sauce for Bolognese or pizza topping and freeze in bags so we can have a taste of summer even on a winters day. I am looking forward to digging some new potatoes at the end of the month; these are the pleasures of growing your own. While our broad beans are coming into season, I'll leave you with my Broad bean starter.

BROAD BEAN STARTER

Heat 200mls. Double cream with a bruised
clove of garlic. Leave to infuse until cold.
Blanch 250g. fresh broad beans in boiling
water for 1 min, drain and blitz in processor
with garlic and cream and two eggs, salt
and pepper, savoury, thyme or marjoram.
Pass mixture through a sieve and pour into
buttered moulds. Bake in a baine Marie in a
moderate oven for 30 mins.

Enjoy your flora and fauna.

JUNE

In the wild larder now a favourite of mine, which is so versatile, is the Elderflower. The flowers need to be picked on a warm dry day then the full heady perfume is evident. I'll give you a recipe for my elderflower fritters at the end.

Everyone knows of elderflower lemonade and elderflower champagne; incidentally, both are made the same way, but for champagne you would add more sugar then leave the natural yeast to convert your sugar to ALCOHOL!!!

The flowers also go very well with early green gooseberries and make a good jam. Earth, or Pig Nuts, can found now (Conopodium majus). It's actually a tuber up to the size of a chestnut, most delicious. These must be dug out of the ground, just follow the slender stem down. (Well worth the effort.)

A swarm of bees in June is worth a silver spoon.

This year seems like a bumper year for rabbits, they can be seen in numbers, half-grown youngsters playing in the fields and on the verges, innocent of passing cars, etc.

By the way, the badger is back. Despite the fences it has found a way around and under them, and its costing poor May Day next door a fortune in fencing panel repairs. Some of the early bird nesters have had their second brook now and are looking less immaculate, while in June the spotted flycatcher, etc, is just thinking of starting.

CUT YOUR THISTLES BEFORE ST. JOHN
(24th JUNE).
YOU WILL HAVE TWO INSTEAD OF ONE.

We are starting to enjoy the rewards of our earlier labours now.

The delights of digging our "new" potatoes, picking young broad beans, peas, salads, etc., in fact an early taste of things to come in the months ahead. We are still planting and sowing outside with our tomatoes, courgettes, peppers, aubergines, celery and squashes, in fact there is always something to plant or harvest.

In the flower garden we have had the first flush of roses and now the herbaceous perennials are in full bloom. Hanging baskets are in place and growing by the day.

It may be an appropriate time to remind our villagers that the Flower Show Committee and our local Avery Plant Centre offer prizes at the show for the best hanging baskets in the village. This is to encourage us to beautiful out surroundings, so let's all try.

When the broad beans and early potatoes are harvested we turn the ground and replant with winter sprouts, kales, cauliflowers, swedes and turnips for our winter crops.

ELDERFLOWER FRITTERS

Take two or three heads of flowers per person
(picked when dry.)
Make a batter using –

Plain flour 125g
Caster sugar 25g
1tbsp. Brandy and 150ml water
add t tbsp oil

Whisk until a thickish batter is obtained. Leave
to rest for half an hour.

When ready, whisk two egg whites until soft
peaks, then fold them into the batter. Take the
flower heads and dip them into the batter.

Fry in hot oil, a few at a time, turning until
golden brown and puffed up.

Keep warm then dredge with caster sugar or
drizzle with honey and serves with lemon
wedges.

Enjoy your flora and fauna.

JULY

St. SWITHINS DAY IF THERE BE RAIN
FOR FORTY DAYS IT WILL REMAIN
St. SWITHINS DAY IF THOU BE FAIR
FOR FORTY DAYS 'TWILL RAIN NAE MAIR

In the wild larder at the moment there is the possibility of finding my favourite mushrooms that is the cep, porcini, penny bun, call it what you will (boletus edulis), for which all of our European partners go wild. They can be purchased for approx. £40. Kilo or you can go up onto the Blackdown or Quantock hills in the woods and pick your own. They are so tasty and with a clove of garlic, parsley and olive oil you have a meal fit for a king. With a little knowledge of fungi you can also find the Pied de mouton, or hedgehog mushroom (hydnum repandum), which is also very good. These will be in season for about 7-8 weeks. Lime leaves (young), on brown bread and butter with cream cheese is a delight. While we are talking about the lime tree, their flowers lightly dried, (a small handful to a medium tea pot) makes a very good pale 'China' tea. Now is a good time to dig up some roots of horseradish and stow away some jars of horseradish sauce to have with that beef or smoked fish.

TILL St. JAMES'S DAY IS PAST AND GONE, THERE MAY BE HOPS OR THERE MAY BE NONE

Most of the birds are now starting to moult, having spent all this time rearing young. They can be quite vulnerable if they lose to many feathers at once as they find it difficult to fly properly. Our badger is still visiting nightly. May has had the badger man out from the wildlife centre and having surveyed the problem, and with much thought, left the decision in her hands i.e. Let the badger come and go as and when he pleases (through the hole he made in her fence), put down a daily dose of a smelly substance called renardine or resort to electric fencing. After deliberation the decision was to let him through the last hole he made.

In the garden there is much to enjoy, all the flowers, sweet peas, roses, herbaceous flowers etc. The vegetable plot is very productive now with all the potatoes, broad, French and runner beans, cauliflower, cabbages, courgettes, peas and in the greenhouse tomatoes and peppers etc.

Fruit like all the berries and currants are in season now in fact, we are on the edge of a glut, so now is the time to put some away in store for a leaner time. Talking of which time for my runner bean chutney.

RUNNER BEAN CHUTNEY.

(MAKE PLENTY AS THEY WILL BE BACK FOR MORE)

2 lbs. Runner beans, cubed into ½ inch chunks (after stringing)
5 onions.
1. 1/2 lbs sugar
1.1/2 pints vinegar
1 Tblsp. Ground turmeric
1 Tblsp. Mustard powder
2 Tblsps. Corn flour
1 Tblsp. Salt.

Method; Boil beans and onions until tender in water then drain well.

Add sugar and 1 1/2 pints of vinegar and simmer for 15 mins.

Mix the rest of the vinegar with the dry ingredients and add to the whole and simmer for a further 15 mins.

Put into hot jars, seal and label.

Makes 8 x 1lb. Jars approx.

Enjoy your flora and fauna.

AUGUST

HARVEST HOME

The last stook of corn to be cut was ceremoniously made into a figure, which was dressed in coloured ribbons and known as Harvest Queen or kern Doll (corn dolly), to represent the Goddess of agriculture.

The wild larder now abounds with a feast of goodies such as Blackberries, Whortleberies; Elderberries are also ready from August to October (pick when the berries begin to hang down as opposed to standing upright).

Most of the greens I have mentioned earlier are still with us and usable. Fungus is now coming into its own, there are the field mushroom, boletus, parasol, ink caps and hydnums. We are spoilt for choice.

24th St Bartholomew

if St Bartholomew's be fine and clear
You may hope for a prosperous Autumn that
year.

In the garden we have a glut as there is so much choice, so enjoy the fruits of your labours, enjoy your runner beans, dwarf beans, tomatoes, courgettes, peppers, celery, onions, etc, etc, but don't forget in these days of plenty to put some away for a rainy day.

There are a host of ways to preserve our surplus fruit and vegetables as well as offering surplus to friends and family.

A pot without bacon is like a sermon without St Augustine. (28th.)

Birds are moulting now and they too are feeing well on the glut, and storing fat for the winter and hard times. I see by the Badger's latrine in our walkway, he has been to the Frank Bond Centre and eaten many cherries.

Rabbits are still running amuck at the Silk Mills Road, and we have so many frogs in Mountway lane I am about to build a small pond as we have four living in a preserving pan under our rain barrel.

For a change this month, as I talked about putting some produce by for leaner times, and there is always a lot of Beetroot around at this time of year, I will leave you, (but especially for Tim Hodge) by revealing a recipe that Aunty Mary gave me some time ago.

Aunty Mary's Beetroot Jelly

2lb cooked beetroot (diced)
1 pint white vinegar
12oz white sugar
1 1/2 packets powdered gelatine
black pepper to taste (or other spice)

Mix gelatine with 1/4 pint vinegar.
Dissolve sugar into the rest of the vinegar in a large pan.
Add beetroot and boil for 10 minutes
Meanwhile, melt gelatine on a low heat and mix all ingredients together well.
cool slightly and liquidize.
Pour into hot sterilized jars and seal.

Makes 5 x 1lb jars.

Enjoy your flora and fauna.

SEPTEMBER

*SEPTEMBER   BLOW   SOFT TILL THE
FRUITS ARE IN THE LOFT*

September in the wild larder is one of plenty.
There are many types of mushroom such as the
Penny bun and hedgehog etc. Only a week ago I
had some Chicken of the wood (picked locally),
also there are blackberries, elderberries, and the
best time to pick Hazelnuts is late this month
when the nuts turn brown. Towards the end of the
month the Rowan berries (which make an
excellent jelly to serve with game), are plentiful.
Hops for beer making are abundant along the Silk
Mills road but beware as these are laden with
traffic fumes and lead, so look for cleaner
pickings. Rabbits will be back in our butchers
shop soon and as a seasonal meat takes some
beating.

*September 14th. Holy-Rood or Holy Cross-is a
festival of the exaltation of the cross.*

*THE DEVIL GOES A-NUTTING ON HOLY
ROOD DAY.*

September in the garden brings plenty of
vegetables to choose from except runner beans,
because the hot temperatures this year put an
early end to the crops. If this is the weather we
are to expect due to global warming then we will

have to think about growing more French beans and Mediterranean type vegetables to compensate.

Top fruits e.g. Apples, pears etc. are starting to ripen now, and as we grow the best apples in the world lets try some of our own for example Ashmeads Kernel, Egremont Russet, Ellison's Orange Pippin (you might not find them in the supermarket), so try your local shop, farm shop or farmers market.

September 29th. St Michael

Michaelmas: - The most popular fare to be eaten on this day is a Michaelmas goose as geese are in their prime now.

On Michaelmas day the devil puts his feet on blackberries.

Frogs are plentiful it seems as every evening I sit in the garden and hear them croaking and see them moving around. I hear the trout are not being seen in the rivers in the village as there are mink on the loose, and although the otters are back they generally prefer eels.

With so many mushrooms around (if you can't find any in the wild you can buy several types at the supermarket for example Chanterel, Oyster, Paris brown etc.) I will give you my starter 'Cornucopia de Fungi'.

Flaky Pastry
An assortment of mushrooms,
Approx. 5fl. Oz. double cream
a little chopped parsley
a clove of garlic
a little good flavoured stock
a knob of butter
salt and pepper.

Fry mushrooms in butter until just cooked, add chopped garlic and a little stock and reduce, add parsley, cream and reduce a little more and season. Meanwhile roll pastry thinly and cut into 1" strips wind around horn tins and cook until golden brown.
Remove from tins and stuff generously, letting filling spill out onto the plate.

Enjoy your flora and fauna.

OCTOBER

Now that it is October, don thy woolly smock.

In the wild larder now there is plenty to gather.
Mushrooms abound in variety, and between now
and December moving from field to woods you
can find field Blewits or as we knew them blue
legs, (tricholoma saevum)
And the all violet-coloured wood blewit (T.
nudum), both have a very pronounced mushroom
flavour, so a few go a long way. The parasol
(Lepiota procera) is also a very good mushroom
to eat, but there are so many at the moment like
chanterelle (cantharellus cibarius) with its
beautiful egg yolk colour and the horn of plenty,
lawyers wig, or shaggy ink cap, all very tasty and
much in demand on the continent. The nuts are
well worth collecting if only for Christmas. Save
them in a tin and keep in the cold outside. Nuts
such as hazel, chestnuts, walnuts and even beech
mast. Make the most to of elderberries; they are
good for making jelly, wine and chutneys etc.
Sloes are also used and as a boy I remember I
would pick baskets full for my Grandmother who
said she made wine with them (I since learnt she
made several bottles of sloe gin with them).
Somewhere out there should be bullaces, which
is a wild plum. These are quite bitter until the
frost acts upon them and the sugars are released.

October sees the Pheasant season open, and well hung this is my favourite meat. Pheasant well cooked makes chicken taste like cardboard.
I am sure our local butcher Tim will have a good supply so do try some.
Pike are usually fished for now (on a frosty day) and can be very nice, apart from the bones.

18th. St. Luke   31st. Halloween

In the garden we are going into autumn greens, some kales, Brussels sprouts etc., also once the first frost start we can enjoy our parsnips, Jerusalem and Chinese artichokes and now winter squashes and pumpkins are ready. It is at this time of year that I gather the last remnants of tomatoes, courgettes, peppers, and aubergines. Garlic etc, and make ratatouille for the freezer. Time now to think about planting garlic cloves for next year and soon to sow broad beans. Most of the flowers in the garden are coming to an end except chrysanthemums for this is there best time.

*A GOOD OCTOBER AND A GOOD BLAST
TO BLOW THE HOG, ACORN AND MAST*

The good life seems to good to be true but if you need feeding, the Lord will provide. On holiday in Cornwall with friends we decided to see what was about, so we looked on the seashore.
Looking up at the rocks above us we were

astounded by the amount of mussels that rose up fifteen feet high around us. We picked only some of the very biggest and took them back to our chalet. In the evening we took our fishing rods down the cliffs and fished while our wives collected blackberries. We had caught two nice sea bass and three mackerel. So that evening we had a bucket of Moules mariniere, roasted sea bass and apple and blackberry pie. What a meal and we enjoyed every minute collecting, preparing and eating it.

WHEN THE OAK WEARS HIS LEAVES IN OCTOBER
YOU CAN EXPECT A HARD WINTER.

PHEASANT TERRINE

(One of my Christmas treats).

1 Plump hen pheasant.
12 oz. Lean veal or chicken (minced).
1 lb. Fat belly pork (minced).
8 oz. Chicken or turkey livers. (Minced).
10 oz. Unsmoked bacon, (chopped small). 1
rounded tspn. Salt.
Tspn. mace.
2 garlic cloves, crushed.
1 tspn. ground black pepper.
12 juniper berries crushed.
5 fl. Oz. dry white wine.
1 fl. Oz. Brandy.
Leaves from 2 sprigs fresh thyme.

Bone, skin and cut pheasant into small dice, mix
with all other ingredients. Cover and leave for
several hours to marinate. Pack mixture into a 3-
pint loaf tin or 2 smaller tins cover with foil.

Place in a baine Marie. Bake in a pre heated
oven 150c. For 1 to 2 hrs.

Remove from oven and let stand to cool. Then
place weight on top to press terrine for easier
slicing. Decorate with fresh thyme and juniper
berries.

Enjoy your flora and fauna

NOVEMBER

No leaves, No birds, No vember.

1ˢᵗ. All Saints.

In the wild larder there are still mushrooms to be found, in particular the Blewits (I have picked these with a coating of ice over them) and Parasols
But generally there is not so much readily available.
A few nuts still and berries such as rose hips and haws, crab apples and wild pear can still be found hanging on the limbs, and any this late are usually very ripe and sweet. In the garden we are using Brussels sprouts, autumn cabbage, carrots, parsnips, Chinese and Jerusalem artichokes.
I have just planted out some lettuce plants for winter salads, these I will cloche later. Time to sow broad beans, round seeded peas and garlic. Back in September I planted a couple of pots of potatoes to try for a few 'new potatoes' for Christmas, I will let you know whether they made it.

11ᵗʰ. St. Martin.

It is the day of Martilmasse,
Cuppes of ale should freelie passé
What thought Wynter has begunne,
To push downe the summer sunne.

39

Rabbits and pheasants are available and while in season are well worth using for a welcome change, as are pigeon, partridge, woodcock and venison all of which I use as regular as possible. Trout are now out of season so I will have to wait until next year to try out Fred Yeandle's trout gravadlax recipe (remember to buy some dill seed).

Advent.

Our local nurseryman on the Silk Mills Road was telling me that whilst walking his dog at night, shone his torch into the field opposite and spotted five foxes and a Roe deer then walking on heard a splash in the river and spotted an otter, just recently, so they are out there and just need looking for. Be quiet be patient and when you spot them be thankful, as we have a wealth of wildlife in and around our village. From now on we need to feed our birds to ensure they give us as much pleasure next year as they did this.

St. Andrew the king
Three weeks and three days before Christmas comes in.

Early this month is a good time to pickle for Christmas supper, onions or shallots in spiced vinegar with a little brown sugar to take the edge off the harshness of vinegar (now I am getting older I can't take it).

Pickled pears are a good choice for a change. Back in August when cucumbers were springing up overnight I made some of Delia Smiths spiced pickled cucumber and onion slices, they should be a welcome change.

Next month being December we will be thinking of Christmas and with that in mind I will give a recipe for spiced pickled beef. This was a Victorian speciality and one, which I usually make. It is very nice with some of the pickles and chutneys we make throughout the year. But for now I have a recipe for a cold winters day.

SOMERSET PHEASANT

2 Pheasants, jointed
2oz. Butter
1Tbsp. Flour
2 Desert apples, peeled and sliced
Pint cider.
Salt & pepper.
Pint chicken stock.
1 large onion, chopped.
Chopped parsley.
Pint double cream.
3 sticks celery, chopped.

Brown pheasant joints in butter in a flameproof casserole.

Remove, put in celery, apples, onion and sauté gently until soft. Stir in flour and gradually add cider and stock.

Bring to a boil, season, then put into a blender until smooth.

Return joints to casserole and pour over sauce. Cover and cook 180c. for approx. 1 hour.

Stir in cream just before serving and add parsley garnish.

Enjoy your flora and fauna.
Roy Baker.

DECEMBER

At Christmas play and make good cheer,
For Christmas comes but once a year.

 In the wild larder there is not very good pickings
for those of us who like to browse around and
forage for nature's gifts at this time of year. You
may still see some wild fungi but not in the
quantities, so a mixed mushroom soup or
omelette is as good as it gets and perhaps a few
chestnuts (that the squirrels have not found.) I
went out to pick some chestnuts for the Christmas
turkey stuffing but found this year they are a little
on the small side.
 One may at this time still find the brown and
frosted leaves of the Burdock, under which is a
good sized root which, when cleaned and roasted
is a very tasty meal. We will remember from our
youth, added to dandelion roots and sugar make
the drink Dandelion and Burdock.

6th. St. Nicholas Bishop of Myra died 324.

 The garden is now producing Brussels sprouts,
some kales (not the nasty curly stuff from the
supermarkets). Like cottagers kale and the old
fashioned thousand headed, taste you cannot buy.
Also we have our artichokes, in particular the
Chinese artichoke, which was a Victorian
delicacy. These are small twisted tubers, which

43

are lifted, washed clean then fried in butter. They are fiddly to prepare but are something else to eat. Parsnips are good now we have had some frost to sweeten them.

27ᵗʰ. St. John.

In the fauna department, we know rabbits are everywhere, so do try Delia Smith's, Old English rabbit pie, I can recommend it.

The badgers are quite active at the moment. I had a bag of small squashes on a table under our covered in patio area, and one morning I got up and went outside to find the bag missing. On inspection of the garden found it at the front of the house. The bag had been ripped open, a squash taken out and sampled by the badger and discarded. Also one of my gardening shoes was alongside with a chunk taken out of the leather tongue. So the badger is always on the hunt for food in the area.

The birds are through the moult now and are looking resplendent in their new plumage. We feed the birds daily but at the moment there are so many berries and other foods out there that birds are not so dependant on us but we must carry on feeding to maintain them throughout the winter months. Pheasants are evident now, and in season, so do try some, they are wonderful when they are at their best (Which is now).

21ˢᵗ. The Shortest day.

Well Christmas will soon be here and I have to say it is one of my favourite times of the year. Time to collect the Christmas tree from our local nursery, the Turkey from Tim's (not tiny Tim's), and boughs of Holly etc. from a friendly farmer. Make the terrine, Spiced beef, Raised game pie, Pressed ox tongue, the puddings were made in October together with the mincemeat, pickles and chutneys, sorted.

So what is it all about? I will leave Sue who is much better placed than me to tell, but without this celebration Jesus' birth we would not have the feeling of giving and sharing, belonging and peace.

26th. St. Stephen

As promised last month spiced pickled beef recipe.
One of the great Victorian Christmas dishes.

A 3lb. Joint of brisket, silverside or topside of beef.
1 Oz. Light brown sugar.
1/2 Oz. Black peppercorns.
1/2 Oz. Juniper berries.
1/2 Oz. Allspice.
2 oz. Sea salt
1/8. oz. Saltpetre. (Not vital but gives better colour).

Trim meat into a neat joint, rub all over with sugar and put into a pot with a cover and leave in a cool place for two days turning the meat occasionally and rubbing in the sugar.

Crush the peppercorns, juniper, allspice and mix with salt and saltpeter.
Rub this mix into the meat and leave in pot for a further nine days. During this time you must tend the beef every day, turning it and rubbing the pickle into the flesh.

When complete remove beef and put into a pan and cover with water, to which is added a bay leaf, a carrot and an onion.
Bring to a boil and simmer slowly for about 2 ½. Hours.

When cool, put on a board and press with weights. Will keep in the fridge for a week plus.

Enjoy your flora and fauna and a very happy and peaceful Christmas to you all.
Roy Baker.

RAMBLINGS
OF
A
VILLAGER

2005

Ramblings of a villager, part 1

Well hello again, you probably thought after last years ramblings that my writing career had finished, but I had an e mail from editor Bob to remind me he hasn't received my article for February in the village. Having gone through the explanation, that I had done a year, ie. February-January and must not repeat myself, his prompt reply was try something else as someone who has been around for a long time! I don't know what you have done to deserve punishment so soon but here goes.

It was not until the age of seven that I truly came to village life. At the tender age of three I started school at St. Johns off Castle Street. We had church services on Wednesday's and Father Jennings and Father Saunders came to our school for the other four days to take assembly and religious instruction. We walked to school every day 1 mile there and the same back. I remember taking a banana to school, one for me and one for my teacher Mrs. Allen it was during the war and it was the first banana I had seen! I duly changed to Bishop's Hull school at the age of seven and went into Miss. Luscombes class, a very strict and severe MISS who took an instant dislike to me as I was taught to print my words and she insisted on joined up writing. After that everyone else was great and the best of all was Mr. Winter, he moved mountains for us taking us on outings up to Swindon railway museum, Clarks and

Moreland's leather curing plant, Cadbury's chocolate factory, Wansbourgh paper mills a Roman villa dig at Clevedon, and walking on Exmoor to Dunkery Beacon where he took photos of us. Fifty years later he was cycling past my house and stopped. Young man he shouted, I have a picture here of you on Dunkery Beacon, it's yours if you can tell me who that boy is in the front row (he had all the other names already written in. As soon as I said Michael Carpenter he remembered. He was 85 years old and I thought what a memory considering all the children who went through the school.

We had good times at the school, Christmas party was the only time we had our GASlights on, and at the prizegivings when I was presented with a book for very good work. Mr. Farrant and Miss Lythal two of our governors presented these. Miss Lythal was an elderly Victorian looking lady who lived at Barr House, she dressed always in black from her bonnet to her long black dress and boots, and carried a large black ear trumpet. It was an awe inspiring experience to collect an award and say thank you Miss Lythal, then she would thrust the trumpet toward your mouth and say '' what did he say'' so you had to repeat it.

At the age of 11 years I could join 14th. Taunton Bishop's Hull Scouts. They had no Cubs at that time so I had to go to 20th. Taunton Holy Trinity. Scouting in the village was great fun; we met at the Hut, which is now the site of the crematorium lodge. It was Aunty Mary who used to do our fund raising then (also brought us jam scones etc for our parties). We used to do 'accident type first aid, rescuing people from the pit in the brickyard. I remember once with Tony Drew strapped on a stretcher and the ropes loosened and about half way up, me holding and walking the stretcher up felt the full weight of Tony on my stomach as he slipped through. We were about ¾. Way up and how we hung on and stopped him plummeting to the bottom I don't know to this day.

We had our Church parades once a month to both churches alternately .We also went camping at Bishops Lydeard after pushing our flatbed truck with all our gear on (today we would have had a minibus), we would pitch our tent, light fires, cook several tins of B&V and potatoes. Can you remember B & V, wartime beef and vegetables?

Now, Bob said keep the recipes in and May suggests soups as most people like soups.
So my first recipe is for May:

LEEK AND BLUE CHEESE SOUP

4 or 5 small leeks
2oz. Butter
3-4 oz. Blue cheese
1 1/2 Pints light stock
Cream or milk
Pepper.

Sweat leeks in butter until soft, crumble in cheese, pour in the stock, cover and simmer for thirty mins.

Blitz, taste and season, add cream or milk.

This can be frozen.
Enjoy.

Ramblings of a villager, part 2

Last month I talked of some of my schooldays and scouting in our village. Now my interest in gardening came about when at the age of about eight I befriended one Colin Smith who lived in Netherclay. His father Charlie Smith was a very well known gardener, showman and judge in the area. He kept the Bishop's Hull flower show running from 1925 until he died in the 1990's. My friend didn't like gardening much so as his friend I used to get all the information when Charlie wanted to pass on hints and tips on gardening, and I was encouraged to take cuttings and sow seeds. At Christmas and birthdays I received seed tokens etc. from Mr. And Mrs. Smith.

When I was 11 years old he gave me a greenhouse and then I was into his favourites, fuchsias and pelargoniums. I remember once saying I would like to learn how to bud roses. He then told me that I would have to see his father in law Mr. Rugg who lived then next to the Constitutional Club. He was a big man and very gentle. I remember he took me out looking for rose briers in the hedgerows during October which we took back and planted in his allotment which was then on the Silk Mills road between Bonds Dairy and Lowlands Terrace. In July he showed me how to take the buds off the rose with the aid of a goose quill and bud it onto the rose stock. He also used to grow his own tobacco and 'cure' it. I was treated like one of the family, going on holiday etc. and at Christmas on Boxing Day we would go to the Mersons next to Edwin Bakers bakery. There we played cards for matchsticks. Charlie taught me how to grow veg. Out of season and encouraged me to show at the flower shows, and years later if I beat him he would be the first to say well done.

He also took me out judging in the latter years to do my ''apprenticeship'' as he called it. Then at the age of 80 odd he said well it's high time you went on your own, and he retired from judging after something like 60 years. I took over his 'round' and have done them ever since. When I was invited to his 90th. Birthday at the Bond Centre he said to me ''keep the flower show going as I have since 1925'' and those words still ring in my ear today. I was sowing seeds a few days ago as it is time to sow our tomato seeds and peppers etc. for some early crops in the greenhouse.

Sweet peas are potted up and quite a lot of seeds can go in outside now, like cabbage, sprouts, lettuce, parsnip, beet, and carrot etc. Flower seeds too, direct into the ground with hardy annuals like pot marigolds, poppies, cornflowers, toadflax, all those old cottage garden plants, whilst on the warmth of a windowsill asters, busy lizzy, petunia etc. can be sown.

I well remember the Rev. Mullins used to show every year and to my knowledge never won a prize. He would bring in his onions, which he grew lovingly then he would 'get them ready for the show bench', which after many times of explaining never quite put into practice his newly attained knowledge. And so he would skin them and trim them then he would say ''why didn't I get a prize they look good enough to eat and I would say that's the problem they are ready to eat and good they look to. But he would be back next year exactly the same. He did try.

As deadline date is beckoning fast and so is Bob, I will get on with my recipe for the month.

CHICKEN PUDDING

Half a fresh chicken
1/2 Lb. button mushrooms
2 oz. Ham
1 tblsp. Chopped parsley
1 oz. Flour
1/2 Pint of chicken stock.

SUET CRUST.
8oz. S.R. flour
4 oz. Suet.
Salt and pepper.
Water to mix.

Take chicken off the bones and toss in seasoned flour, chop mushrooms and ham.
Mix suet crust together and line a basin.

Layer chicken, ham, parsley and mushrooms, season well, pour in stock, fix lid and steam for three hours.

Serve with broccoli and new potatoes.

Enjoy!

Ramblings of a villager, part 3

Before I close the chapter of Bishop's Hull
Flower Show, I would like to recall a time in the
1960's, when Mrs. Smith 'encouraged' my wife
Margaret to show in the home craft section of our
show. She proudly took her exhibits into the old
school and left them to be judged. Whilst as
secretary I went to record who won what, Aunty
Mary Drew was heard to say to Mrs. Smith,
''look Olive 1st. for Madeira, 1st, for jam tarts,
and 1st. for Victoria sponge, who is this Baker
woman, whereupon Mrs. Smith said 'it's our
Roy's wife Margaret, and aunty Mary said 'O
thank goodness it is one of our own, for a minute
I thought it was an outsider'. That was in the days
when Bishop's Hull was quite a bit smaller and
everyone knew everyone else. I actually met my
wife in the village, outside of the scout hut when
I helped with the cubs, some 47 years ago we
have been married now 42 years.
Remembering the times we were lads here, takes
me back to the fields which are now Gillards,
Waterfields Drive, Bakers close and Jarmyns etc.,
Fields where we earnt money picking Peas and
Broad Beans at, 1/6d per sack of peas and 9d. for
a sack of broad beans. We would stay in the
fields all day sometimes to earn much needed
money, only breaking to go over the road to the
Bakers Mr. Tucks on the Wellington road where
the Esso garage is now , to get a loaf of bread to

eat. It went down lovely all hot and greyish colour. There was a footpath which went across the fields there to the five bar gate behind the 'New' Vicarage now an entrance to the village field.

As a lad there were a number of farms in the village and names like Diamonds, Venn's, Biffen, Quartly, and Gregory spring to mind and we would arrange to meet at Quartly's barn or at panney which was the river below Roly Poly, in Frank Bonds field where the old Cricket Pavilion was. Names I hadn't heard for years were (and I wonder how many people remember), Fan Dance Hill, Pigs loose Lane, and 18 acres, Iron Bridge, Old Canal and Malt house. We would wait outside Church on a Sunday evening for our girlfriends to come out and the old village Bobby P.C.Rex would arrive on his bike and say 'move along lads, you'll end up into trouble hanging around here, now be off with you'. We did not need a second telling as it was in the days when you might get a thick ear.

Well April is here and Easter is nigh, a very significant time in the Church. It is also a time when I think of my early days with walks to the woods to pick primroses with Marmite sandwiches and ginger beer or homemade lemonade. Simnel cakes decorated with crystallized primroses and Easter eggs made with dark chocolate (that was all there was available) and decorated with crystallized violets etc.

I feel I should mention garden task's at this time but time and editor Bob is looming so, while asparagus is coming into season I will give you my recipe for,

QUAIL EGGS, ASPARAGUS AND GOAT CHEESE TARTS

Line 6 small tart tins with short crust pastry and bake blind.
Boil 6 quail eggs in water for about 1 minute, then cool.
Blanch in boiling water for 4 mins. 8 asparagus spears then refresh in cold water.

Make a custard using 1 whole egg and 1 egg yolk, a little cream and a little milk. Season with salt and pepper and beat to mix.

Now shell the quail eggs and slice in half, chop the spears into 3 or 4 pieces place these with the halved eggs into the tarts. Crumble some goats cheese on top and pour on the custard. Dust with a little cayenne pepper and bake in a moderate oven for approx. 20 mins.

This makes a good starter. I hope you will try it,
Enjoy.

Ramblings of a villager, part 4
May

I live in what was once the kitchen garden To
Mountway House. As I dig my garden the soil
had been worked by generations of gardeners, as
they grew the veg for the "house" it shows the
work they put in because the good topsoil goes
down at least 2 feet and I am always turning up
Blue and White china pieces. The house was said
to be haunted and over the years fell into
disrepair. I remember once as a lad, my friend
and me went to see if we could see any ghost and
when we went into the shade of the oak trees we
heard a piano playing. On further investigation
and peeping through the boarded window we
saw, not a ghost but a village lad playing the
piano, we were relieved. The house was
eventually demolished and bungalows were built
in the 50s.
 Once in a while Frank Bond would open his
gardens to the village and show off his collection
of aviary birds, glasshouses with begonias etc.
and his wonderful collection of organs. Some
were fairground type Wurlitzer organs, blaring
out old tunes with their backing drums and
cymbals. People would buy a tea and sit down
and listen or join in the singing. Then a beautiful
sound would come from an organ, really melodic
and a tune that would make the hair stand on end.
One such tune I remembered was 'in a Monastery

garden', and then as a finale would lead the singing of hymns like the Old Rugged Cross. The money raised would go to a charity and once to the Flower show of which he was the President.

Just prior to writing this, I was sowing some herb seeds of basil, dill and coriander, I need to grow some dill as I must get Fred Yeandle's recipe for Gravadlax, so when I catch a big trout I will be able to try it. By the way, when I wrote in February describing a meal that I 'caught, grew, brewed etc. which I related cost me nothing but it was a meal fit for a king' I mentioned that had I had a cow there might be cheese to finish, well I might add that it sparked something in me that said why not make cheese. So I fashioned a sort of cheese press out of chopping boards and some dowel, made moulds out of large fruit tins and a friend turned me some oak 'followers' on his lathe, and with a chat to a cheesemaker, I am the proud owner of three maturing cheeses. I have sent away for some culture of Penicillin Roquforti then I can make 'blue cheese. I am now making my own butter. So there you have it, home made bread, butter and cheese, not to mention Piccalilli and parsnip wine blackberry wine and grape wine. My very own cheese and wine party.

Now we are in May we can towards the end of the month think about putting into the garden the tomatoes, peppers, courgettes and those frost tender plants including runner beans. Some of you who go to the Good Companions, may have a few tomato plants that I asked you to try, well the end of the month is the time to plant them outside, and I am sure you will enjoy your own grown toms, they will be better than you can buy, anywhere.

 I might mention that we (the flower show committee) have a social evening on the 21st May in the Church hall, it's a free evening and everyone is invited. It's an American supper, we supply the teas, and Fred puts on a plant stall so you may find that plant you are looking for.

 Well it's time for a recipe and I would like you to try my,

CHEESE, TOMATO AND ONION BREAD.

1lb. Strong white flour.
1-teaspoon salt
1 Sachet easiblend yeast
10fld. Oz. Water into which,
1 tblsp. Tomato puree.
3oz. Grated cheese.
1/2 grated onion
1 or 2 chopped sun dried tomatoes.

Mix all ing. in a bowl, put onto a floured worktop and knead until the dough is 'elastic'(I was taught to knead 65 times). Put into an oiled poly bag to prove until the dough has doubled in size. Knock back and put into a loaf tin or shape it into a ball, and put on a baking sheet.

Leave to prove again until twice the size.

Brush with beaten egg and put into pre-heated oven at 200c. for approx. 30 mins.

Knock the base to see if done, it should sound hollow.

Do have a go and tell me what you think.

Enjoy.

Ramblings of a villager, part 5.
June

We were very privileged last month to be invited to a surprise 80th. Birthday party of a very well known villager, who's name is almost a legend. He has worked tirelessly over many years to the benefit of the Cricket team which he maintained for years and played for, the Flower show which he has again put in a lot of work time and effort to keep it going, The Frank Bond Centre, not to mention Clatworthy Fly fishing club. He has held post in all of these organisations.

We are of course talking of Fred Yeandle. Well at 80, Fred is tireless in his approach and looks very much like continuing to use his skills to good advantage.

It was testament to Fred to see the many relatives and friends that came to celebrate with him, from as far away as Australia. We were also well fed and "watered" by his son Niel and daughter Denny, and I would like to say a personal thanks to Fred and Jo for their help and support with the, Flower show and for being a great mate.

Well flaming June is here and we are probably thinking of warm summer evenings, bar-b-ques etc. and as I sit under the canopy of grape vines laden with swelling grapes I wonder should I make some more grape wine this year. Last year I made 1 gallon and the blackbirds were allowed to have the rest. Seems a waste and I hate waste so I will make more. One blackbird in particular with a scruffy tail "Blackie " has become addicted to the grape so about three or four times a day comes into the house for her raisons. She will come into the conservatory or sit on the window ledge until I get up and feed her outside with her ration. She has got so tame and will come onto the table and take her raisons. On May 8th. She came and presented two youngsters.

We are now planting out our tomatoes, courgettes, cucumbers, busy lizzies, geraniums etc. now the fear of frost should be past.

Most things in the garden are looking well and tasting even better. It is a satisfying feeling to go into the garden and pick up a complete salad, come inside and eat it within minuets. What a difference from toms. from Holland, lettuce from Spain, beetroots from South America and spring onions from probably Timbuktu.

How many hours in travel time alone, before it gets a bed on a supermarket shelf? This good life is a real possibility and could as easily be yours.

With the warm summer evenings on us I like to sit out and reminisce of times past and one thing that came to me the other night was hot summers of youth and 'GINGER BEER' So to end this months Ramblings I will leave a recipe for ginger beer (a nice cooling drink).

GINGER BEER.

1 Lemon
1/2 Oz.Dried root ginger, bruised
1/2 Oz. Cream of tartar
1 1/2 Lbs. Loaf sugar
1 gallon water
1/2 Oz. Dried yeast

Peel lemons, squeeze and strain the juice , and
put both in a bowl.

Add the well bruised ginger, the cream of tartar
and the sugar.

Pour on the boiling water and allow to stand
until just warm, then add the frothed yeast.

Stir well together, cover with a cloth, leave in a
warm place overnight.

Next day skim off the yeast and bottle
immediately, using strong bottles.

This can be used at once, but is better if allowed
to remain undisturbed for three days.

Enjoy!

Ramblings of a villager, part 6.
July

We are in the second end of the year now and as
I write this I am thinking that only a few weeks
ago the Bishop's Hull flower show committee
had its annual Social evening in the Church hall.
How lucky we are as a village to have 'ladies'
that will turn up and 'do' teas etc. as a matter of
course. They are not committee members but will
help out without question when required. The
evening was a great success and many villagers
went home with plants they had bought, some
indeed given freely by our very own plant centre
owner Allen Avery who also gave us an
informative talk on new plants and how to look
after them, with an emphasis on watering
correctly.
  There is a poem which says you are closer to god
in a garden, than anywhere else on earth, and any
gardener at some time feels this without doubt.
You only have to see seeds sprouting into
beautiful flowers or fine vegetables and it
gladdens the heart. You can also see how the
elements affect the growth of plants and the
diversities of plants, and you are in awe of the
greatness of it. Gardening is a wonderful job,
pastime, life and you are at one with nature and
the giver of life.
  As an artisan provider of food and all things
edible, I would inform you that my cheese

making experiments worked very well, and many friends came once the cheese was cut and had a taster. It was deemed a success by all but one who thought it was a 'bit too strong' Also my first real try at brewing beer turned out very well and is now known as "BISHOP'S ALE" a good bitter. I think by Christmas, last years "Mountway Merlot" may be ready to try. We have been picking tomatoes, asparagus, potatoes, broad beans and salads etc. and about the 15th. Of the month I shall be picking runner beans, that means summer is truly here, any surplus is given to neighbours, made into chutney etc. but certainly not wasted.

We are planning this years Flower show and I have often thought, wouldn't it great if we could all get together and have a Village Day, with Flower show, Fete, dog show, bar-b-q. dance in the field etc. as some other villages do. A pig roast and square dance, flower festival the possibilities are endless, when the whole village comes together.

Now is the time of year to plant out all those winter greens, sprouts, purple sprouting broccoli kales, savoy and spring cauliflower. There is always something to do in the garden but at this time of year it is a good time to just relax and enjoy the fruits of your labours. And in the evening a bar-b-q, a few friends and put the world to rights.

Well I was going to give a recipe with summer overtones but with a bar-b-q. in mind my recipe using a plethora of adjectives for.

BAR-B-Q. MARINADE FOR CHICKEN OR PORK.

In a bowl put a handful of dark brown sugar, a squirt of tomato puree, a fair dollop of tomato sauce, a smidgen of mustard, a good trickle of honey, a shake of salt, a grind or two of black pepper, a couple of drips of Tabasco, or two shakes of Worcester sauce.

Mix all the ingredients together and throw in your chicken pieces or pork and massage them. Cover in clingfilm and leave in the fridge until ready to cook.
Cook on BAR-B-Q. turning regularly.
Very tasty.

Enjoy.

Ramblings of a villager, part 7
August

August is here, and in the garden it's a time of
plenty. We have at our disposal, runner beans,
beetroots, tomatoes, dwarf beans, carrots,
courgettes, peppers, aubergines, cucumbers etc,
etc, and we feel contented that we have worked at
providing for ourselves and now we are reaping
our rewards. Those of you who grow flowers, fruit
and vegetables and also do handicrafts etc. can
show your efforts in the forthcoming flower show
on the 14th. August. Just pick up a schedule in the
butchers or phone Fred or myself for one, last
years exhibitors has already had one delivered. We
do try to beautify our village by encouraging you
to put up a hanging basket or tubs, we then judge
them and our local Plant centre, and us, give
money prizes to the top three in each category.
  A walk around the village now will tell you that in
nature, the time of plenty is here as blackberries
are fruiting, hazelnuts are nearly ready, as is the
hops. Fungi and many more of the natural larder is
at our disposal. It is fair to say that I eat well both
from home made, home grown and wild foods and
enjoy regularly from the freezer, rabbits, pheasant,
pigeon, venison and all rod caught sea fish and
trout. Last month, I managed to get Fred Yeandle's
trout gravadlax recipe from him. Well it is a very
good recipe and one which I shall continue to use
over and over again. Imagine trout marinading in

sea salt, brown sugar, black pepper, mustard, lime zest and juice and dill weed for 4 days, then sliced thinly, it was fantastic, so thanks Fred it was well worth waiting for.

On the subject of food (which I am seldom off) I made a beautiful soft goats cheese the other day which I rolled in chopped soft herbs which went down well and also a darker, stronger 'Bishop's Ale' which has now been bottled. We should see in the woods and the fields now many mushrooms like cep, hedgehog, chanterelle and field mushroom, a veritable feast for the likes of me.

Still on the subject of food, and in particular my recipe for ginger beer. I owe a public apology to Joyce Robinson who rang me before going on holiday to Sicily asking about the said recipe as she was going to take the ingredients with her to make whilst on holiday. She asked me whether to skin the ginger or not, I really wasn't thinking and said "just give it a good bashing to bruise it well. What I did not realise was in my recipe I use dried root ginger and hadn't specified this. So Joyce was on her way and suddenly I realised that she was probably using fresh root ginger and the amount would not have given enough flavour. So a public apology Joyce I am indeed very sorry.

August reminds me of outings we had as children at Bishop's Hull school, in particular Mr. Winter our schoolteacher took us walking on the moor at

Dunkery and on the Quantocks out to Wills neck and back to West Bagborough.

We would pick and eat whortleberries until our hands and mouth was purple, it was great to walk miles, and by the time we got to the bus stop at the top of Buncome Hill, we were tired out, ragged and purple. I don't know what the bus driver thought of us. I didn't realise until years later that Mr. Winter used to pay our fares from his own pocket. He was a very good teacher and on reflection he was a strong disciplinarian, but always very fair and helpful. I saw him regularly over the years and until his death, he still called me 'young man', I still called him 'sir', not quite the way it happens today but he always demanded and got respect, willingly.

Looking up the pole at my Fuggles hop plant the other day, reminded me of the Hops that grow along the hedges at Silk Mills road, and years ago Hops were grown in the village, presumably for the Malthouse in the village to make beer. There is so much to see in our village when you are out and about and lots more to find out.

For now that's about it and so on to my monthly recipe. (I must get it right). As I make a lot of tomato soup when the glut comes, here is my soup recipe:

FRESH TOMATO SOUP.

1 lb. Fresh tomatoes (skinned and quartered)
1 large onion chopped
1 large potato cubed
1 pint of veg or chicken stock
some basil leaves
olive oil and salt and pepper
1 tablespoon tomato puree
2 garlic cloves
2 teaspoons sugar
a good dash of Worscester sauce

Put oil in a pan and sauté onions and garlic then add potatoes and sauté for a few mins. .
Add tomatoes, stock, tomato puree, basil leaves and seasoning and simmer for 30 mins.
Put into a blender and blitz until creamy.
Add cream to serve topped with cheesy, garlicky croutons.

Good hot or cold and freezes well without cream.

Enjoy.

Ramblings of a villager, part 8.
September

I must start this months ramblings by mentioning
the passing of a very dear friend of some thirty
odd years, our very own May Day. May was a
true villager in every sense of the word other than
she was not born in the village. In her long life
she was a Churchgoer, link lady, Good
companions chairman, Flower Show Treasurer,
Townswomans Guild committee member, Wine
Guild Chairman, friend to many, councillor to
very many, helper to the helpless and hopeless.
May was a mine of information, she would not
suffer fools gladly. It was a privilege to know
May, and I know it's a cliché but they broke the
mould when she was born. I will miss her
immensely.
Well September is here, the season of mellow
fruitfulness and talking of which, what a season.
Very hot, very dry, very wet, very wearing. We
have been putting crops by for a rainy day, like
freezing broad beans and peas. We have been
making tomato sauce with the glut of toms, also
piccalilli with the spare runner beans, courgettes,
shallots and caulis, greengage jam, greengage
wine and black grape wine (Mountway Merlot). I
have quite a good crop of Hops to pick in and
dry. It goes well with crystal malt and makes a
good ale which costs 15p per pint to make. Real
ale at 15p, that takes you back doesn't it.

Many of you came to the Flower Show and made it a cracking success. It was nice to see and speak to so many of you. Our President Lady Skelmersdale gave a speech and duly awarded the cups and special prizes. She was presented with a posy of flowers by prizewinner 6 year old Christina Schoonakker. We were visited by the M.P. for Taunton Adrian Flook and his wife Frangelica. Lady Skelmersdale introduced us to them and then photographs were taken for our records.

We also had a visit from Richard Fox from Wellington (late of Fox Bros). Who is the President of Wellington Flower Show. A very nice man who has visited us before and passed comment on the good standard of entries. And while talking of standards, the homecraft judge Mrs. Singleton said " Bishop's Hull has some very good cooks" and that your exhibits were "the best I have judged this year", so pat yourselves on the back.

Your village show was a great social success, plants were bought, raffle tickets went well, Freds auction of produce is always worth watching, lots of tea was consumed and it was nice to see the residents from the Manor Nursing Home having a good time, and one lady in particular Joy Wakefield in open competition won the best handicraft in show with a ceramic piggybank, and went away with the Cup and a £5. voucher. And so I say thank you all for making it a great day, and thank you Sue for supporting us.

Well Bob is on his way to the wedding and I must not waffle on any more or he will be late.

So to my recipe, May loved soups and this was her favourite, so here goes.

CELERY AND STILTON SOUP.

2 Heads of celery chopped
1 onion   "
2 Potatoes   "
1 Carrot   "
2 Cloves garlic   "
1 Pint milk
1 Pint water
Salt, pepper, a little oil or butter
2 Stock cubes, veg, or chicken
Stilton cheese , crumbled
Bay leaf, parsley and thyme.

Sweat onions, garlic, celery and carrots in oil until soft but not coloured.

Add potatoes, milk, water, salt, pepper, stock cubes and herbs.

Bring to boil then simmer for approx. 30 mins. (until veg is tender).

Put soup through a blender, reheat and serve.

Put stilton into bowls, apportion of celery leaf if possible to decorate and a swirl of cream if desired.

Makes approx. 3 pints.

Enjoy.

Ramblings of a villager part 9
Oct.

October is here and this is a good time of the year for the forager and wild food enthusiast as game is in season, and a visit to Tim's our butcher will show what is about now.

Pheasants, rabbits etc. a time of plenty. Who could resist a nice roasted pheasant, full of flavour or a roasted or stewed rabbit. Come on when did you last try one. During and after the war we lived on them as a supplement to our ration, and now, well I still think they are fantastic.

I remember my Mother used to, it seemed always have a rabbit stew on the hob. I could come in with a schoolmate and there was a meal fit for a king, dished up any old time of day. We would go down the road and buy a rabbit for sixpence, and when the rag and bone man came around we would get 3d.back on the skin.

We always kept chickens, ducks, and a couple of geese for Christmas and an occasional half pig. So with the aforesaid rabbits and occasional pheasants, pigeon's etc. we were very well 'fed', then we had the butchers few slices of corned beef, liver and so on. I remember as a schoolboy going into the restaurant in the Victoria rooms in town and you paid for tokens, red = gravy and so on, well I had with the appropriate tokens, rabbit pie, greens, potatoes, carrots and gravy. It was good and the smell of that restaurant is still with me today.

I think this is why I am what I call an artisan provider of food. I am constantly on a quest to make items like butter, bread, cheese, chutney, pickles, sausages, faggots, and bacon etc. etc. I just love to make them and a feeling of contentment and fulfillment comes over me when I have done a good job of it. When I go into the wild and find mushrooms, nuts, berries, roots and shoots etc. and make a good meal of them I feel like I am using the store nature intended for us.

In the garden we are still picking beans, beet, tomatoes, peppers and leeks, the kales are not yet with us. Some of the bulbs are pushing through in the flower garden, with a promise of fulfillment in the Spring, and a few such as the nerine are flowering now. Fruit needs to be picked in now and stored, and I like to poach some hard pears in syrup and bottle for later, as they remind me of Sunday teas when I was a lad with condensed carnation milk on them.

Most of the wild fruit and nuts are just about over now (you may be lucky and find some chestnuts) But what a harvest when they were around. I picked 12lbs. Of elderberries for wine and blackberries were abundant. There should still be some mushrooms around now, (I have had my share this year) I have had giant puffballs field mushrooms, horse mushrooms and soon I hope blewits.

I really must go in and see our village wood. I think it's a very good facility for us and in years to come it will be good to stroll around and watch it develop. I wonder how long it will be before we see foxgloves, bluebells and wood anemones etc. there. I am sure such will be planted in the fullness of time also wild mushrooms will settle and wild life in general will take refuge there and so we will have a natural wooded environment to add to this beautiful village of ours.

So now to my monthly recipe and this month being October and the thought of winter ahead, a nice warming rabbit casserole (what else).

RABBIT CASSEROLE.

1 rabbit jointed. (see Tim).
2 carrots chopped
2 sticks of celery chopped
1 small turnip chopped
1 onion chopped
1 leek chopped
2 rashers of streaky bacon diced
1 pint of stock, or half cider, half stock
a little flour
sliced potatoes for the topping
a few sprigs of thyme and a bay leaf
salt and pepper

Dust rabbit with seasoned flour, brown in lard, remove from pan, add bacon and brown, add vegetables and lightly brown.

Now return rabbit, add stock, herbs and seasoning.

Lay the slices of potato over the top in tile fashion, overlapping, dot with butter, cover with a lid and put into a preheated oven 160 F. for 1½ - 2 hours, remove lid for last 10 mins. to brown potato.

Enjoy.

Ramblings of a villager, part 10
November

When I was a lad in my early teens, square
dancing was quite a big thing and we used to go
to the square dance nights in the old Village Hall,
beside and behind the butchers shop in the
village. Miss Reed (the school bank lady), called
the dances to the music of records. Dances, the
names of which I can hardly remember now, but
names like 'Waltz country dance', 'Valletta',
'Gay Gordons' 'Dip and Dive' etc. were the
order of the day. It was about threpence old
money, which included a soft drink and was a
good night out, boys and girls from the village
would fill the hall every time. We would then get
invited to Bishop Fox's school square dances and
that was really something else. We eventually
grew older and then went to the big dances at the
Empire and Dellers in town and later at the T.A.
hall in the village.

After last months ramblings talking about the
season of game meats and prompting you to our
butcher Tim, I thought I would see what he had
and to my delight, there painted on the window
was Fresh venison, rabbits and pheasants just as I
had predicted, well done Tim. Whilst on the
subject of butchers, it will soon be time to order
our Christmas poultry. I am always in a quandary
as what to order, should it be our usual turkey or
a goose for a change. I do like goose very much,
but when the family is together a goose doesn't

go far enough, but the richness of the meat is beautiful. One year I filled the cavity with apples and prunes soaked in Grand Armangnac and the sauce it made was heavenly.

Geese were traditionally Christmas fare and as a lad we kept two geese especially for our dinner as there were six of us and you needed two to go around, then often for Boxing Day we would roast two or three stuffed rabbits in the goose fat and they tasted beautiful.

There is not much in the wild larder other than game to keep body and soul together except a few mushrooms like blewits or oysters at the moment. Thank goodness for the garden as we can now feed on the kales, winter cabbage, leeks, sprouts parsnips, etc. The runner beans I started to pick on the 9th. July have just about finished. What a crop! They kept coming until that very dry very hot period we had and I thought that was the end, but I stripped off all of the shriveled beans, gave them a good feed of fish, blood and bone meal, a few good waterings and they came back with a vengeance.

I started making Bacon last month and it proved to be a very successful exercise. With a piece of belly pork, some salt, saltpetre and brown sugar, a beautiful dry cure bacon was made and all who tried it said 'YES' and so another fortnightly regime is set into place. I am going to try a ham and also although I do some hot smoking, I would like to cold smoke, bacon, trout, eel, etc.

so am looking for appropriate metal furniture to make a cold smoker.

In November one thinks of bonfire night and fireworks, and we always had particular food for the occasion which usually consisted of potatoes roasted in the embers of the fire together with sausages and pumpkin soup. This has prompted me to leave you with my recipe for roast pepper and pumpkin (I use butternut squash) soup. Also pumpkin pie for those of you with a sweet tooth.

ROAST RED PEPPER AND PUMPKIN SOUP.

Cut a butternut squash into 8 lengthways and quarter and deseed 2 red peppers.

Toss with a little olive oil and roast with 3 whole garlic cloves for approx. 45 mins. In a hot oven.

Cool, discard skins, deglaze roasting pan, add veg to pan with ¾. Pint of stock.

Bring to boil and blitz with a blender.

Add a little cream and a few knobs of butter, season to taste, stir and serve.

PUMPKIN PIE

8 oz. Pastry
1 lb. Raw pumpkin
2 Eggs

1/2 Pint evaporated milk
4 oz. Soft brown sugar
1 teaspoon cinnamon powder
1/2 Teaspoon ground ginger
1/2 Teaspoon Nutmeg

Cut up and cook pumpkin in water until soft then blitz.

Break and beat eggs and add evaporated milk, pumpkin puree, sugar, spices and mix well.

With pastry make individual tartlet cases or one large flan.

Spoon mixture into tartlet cases and bake in a preheated oven 190c. for 20-30 mins.

Serve hot or cold with cream.

Enjoy.

Ramblings of a villager, part 11
December.

Is it really 12 months ago that I suggested you
ordered you're turkey and got you're Christmas
tree etc? Well here we are again in the thick of
Christmas preparation.
 Christmas cake, mincemeat, several puddings,
pickles, chutneys, cheddar cheese, stilton cheese,
beer, wine all made and still pressed ox tongue,
pheasant pate and savoury biscuits to make.
 I really love this time of giving and sharing,
carols and goodwill. It's a time as well for family
traditions, and getting together. It's a time too for
celebrating the birth of Christ. Christmas is also a
time to remember your youth, the good times you
had, the parties. All that and more, wrapped up in
a couple of days, so why do we need all this
preparation? We just like to give our family and
friends a good time and see them happy, after all
it is a celebration.
 The wild larder still provides game such as
rabbits, pheasants, and various mushrooms can
still be found. Only a couple of weeks ago I
picked blewits , shaggy ink caps and parasols.
The garden is producing kales, my favourite
greens, cabbages, and leeks, etc. it all
compliments the seasonal game. Garden flowers
are still trying their best too, kaffir lilies and
nerines etc. still flowering to brighten the day as
does penstemons and I still have a pink out in
flower.

There is still time to plant bare root trees and shrubs; I am planting some fruit trees on a fence to provide a few apples, pears and figs for the future. We can always find space for something we can go out and pick and enjoy.

We have had our first frost and that put an end to runner beans and put the dahlias to sleep but it will sweeten Brussels sprouts and parsnips as when they have been frosted the starches in parsnips are turned into sugars and this makes them much sweeter.

There are out there masses of berries, holly, cotoneaster, crateagus or hawthorn which as we all know heralds a hard winter. There are also reports of record numbers of redwings, waxwings and the like, (another sign of hard weather). Squirrels have been very active storing nuts and berries, do they know something? But still the weathermen say nothing to worry about. Only the fullness of time will tell who has got it wrong, I hope it's Mother Nature but I have been wrong before.

Last year we made our mincemeat for our pies with real meat in the shape of minced beef, the tarts were very nice and not over sweet, quite a change, you might say but apparently this was the original mincemeat. So this year I thought you might like to try, as it is very nice I promise.

REAL MINCEMEAT.

Makes about three 1lb jars

250g. finely minced lean beef
125g. beef suet.
125g. currants.
125g. raisins
250g tart eating apples finely chopped
100g. soft brown sugar.
65g. ground almonds
50g. preserved ginger finely chopped and
2 tablespoons syrup from jar
50g. mixed candied peel chopped
grated zest and juice of 1/2 Lemon
grated zest and juice of 1/2 orange
1/2 Teaspoon nutmeg
1 teaspoon ground mixed spice
125ml. Rum or brandy.

Put all ingredients in a bowl and mix
thoroughly with your hands.
Put into a jar and seal. Keep in a cool
place for up to 1 month before using.
Pop into pastry cases, glaze and cook in
pre heated oven 180c. for 15 – 20 mins.

I would like to wish you all a very happy,
healthy, peaceful Christmas and new year.
Enjoy, Roy Baker.
Ramblings of a villager, part 12

January, 2005.

A very happy, healthy and peaceful New Year to you all.

Well another year has passed by. I have written two pages per monthly magazine for two years now and my "Ramblings" are in serious threat of becoming Wafflings, so before that happens I shall take a break from regular monthly writings to an occasional article. I thank you all for putting up with my thoughts and ideals over the last 2 years and wish you well.

I have since I last wrote, made two very different black puddings, one was a dried blood mix with added seasonings and the other, the real thing. It was a messy operation to do but I now have some in the freezer to go with my dry cured bacon and sausages. All these home processing skills are well worth the time and effort to do, you pick up ways to do things that you cannot always find in books.

All of these artisan skills are soon learnt and put into practice and as well as taking photographs of the stages of making, I hope sometime to put pen to paper and hopefully end up with a small book I can leave my Children/ Grandchildren so the information is passed on. I have already had three different offers from interested food outlets for my dry cured bacon and cheese, but I am not interested in money making but getting people into trying to make something in the hope it would spur them on to be more self reliant, and one or two I have leaned on are making bacon, sausages and butter, and enjoying the fruits of their labours.

In the garden there are still a good few flowers that brighten the day. Vegetables are still producing and the time has come to start 2005 sowing of seeds like onions and a few very early tomatoes. I have just bought an apple tree, 'Orleans Reinette' a very tasty old French russet variety. We went to Charlton Orchards apple tasting day on Saturday 4th Dec. I had been looking for years for this tree so I had to buy one, and a couple pounds of fruit to remind myself of the taste.

In the wild there is not much around now, rabbits and pheasant are still with us and I must say I had a few rabbits just before Christmas and made 30 bunny burgers to go into the freezers. It is one way to get children to eat and enjoy them. Pheasants are I think, best enjoyed by stuffing with a sage and onion stuffing, a few streaky bacon rashers on top and roasting. A bird I love when then come my way (about twice in a season) is woodcock. These are cooked and eaten just plucked, and the innards are often spread on toast, it is the most gamey of the bird world and very tasty.

I would like to take this opportunity to offer that if anyone who thought of having a go at making butter, sausages, bacon, faggots, black puddings, beer, wine etc. etc. I have contacts of the necessary ingredients and/ or equipment to see it come to fruition, so just give me a ring or see me and I will help all I can.

Well the time has come for my last recipe of the month and that makes 24, enough for a small book almost!
So I will again thank you for putting up with my Ramblings over the last two years and leave you with a recipe for:

MY FAGGOTS

Pigs liver about 1 1/2 Lbs
1 pigs heart
1 lb. Belly pork
1 lb. Onions
4 oz. Fresh breadcrumbs
10 ish fresh sage leaves chopped.
salt and pepper
pigs caul, to cover if possible.

Cut the meats into large cubes cut onion into four, put into a pan and cover with water, bring to boil and simmer for 1 hour.

Drain liquid and reserve for the gravy. Mince the meats and onion, add chopped sage, breadcrumbs, salt and pepper (don't be meager with the seasoning), and mix thoroughly using a little of the liquid if required.

Grease a baking pan, roll the mix into small cricket balls, cover with caul fat if you can find it, and bake into a preheated oven at 180c. until brown, approx 30 mins.

Make a fine gravy with the cooking liquid and serve with mashed potatoes and mushy peas.

I hope you will try my faggots and for the last time, Enjoy.

Roy Baker.

ARTISAN
COOKING
AND
PROCESSING

2006

An Artisan look at food and cooking, part one.

Back in March, Sue wrote about bringing back real cooking and having a "Be bothered to cook" month.

Did anyone give it a try?

Well I would like to try again but not for a month, but always.

If we look back, we can remember a family gathering around the table for meals, and this was where solutions to problems were resolved, ideas were shared, (along with secrets), hopes and dreams talked over, worries shared we were in fact a family unit that could talk to one another. One hears so many times that dinner is eaten from a tray in front of the box. Where have we gone wrong? It was whilst giving a talk to the 'Good Companions' on artisan cooking and processing that when they tried samples of my processed foods like breads, butter, cheese, sausages, brawn, bacon, beers, wines etc. etc. several said to me "that's what food used to taste like" and why can't we buy stuff like that, and "my Mother used to make this and that." It was then I realised that generally not very many did home processing or indeed with the younger generation very little home cooking from scratch. We see recipe cards at the supermarkets, Take 8oz. Of ****** finest marinated salmon fillets, a ******pre baked flan case etc.etc. and you can cook a meal to remember. Mrs. Beetons recipe would start, 'First catch your fish'. Well I hope I have got you thinking. Next month I will talk about food and where we buy or collect it. I intend to give a recipe each month that is easy to prepare and cook and use 'in season' foods and as peas are in season now I will start with,

PEAS AND HAM IN CREAM.

1.1/2. Lbs. Peas, weighed before shelling or frozen can be used.
1 . oz. Butter
1 medium onion, (thinly sliced.)
1. lb. Ham, cut into slices.
1/2 pint double cream.
10, chopped sage leaves
2 teaspoons of clear honey.

Put peas, onion and butter in a pan, cover and sweat for 10 mins. Add the ham then mix in the sage, honey and cream season and cover again and simmer for 10 mins more. Serve with new boiled potatoes.

Do try, and enjoy it, a very simple but tasty dish.

It's a good life, enjoy it.

Artisan cooking and processing.

Where do we buy our food from? Sainsburys, Tesco, Asda, Morrisons or other large stores, Tims, butchers, P.O. and store, Rumwell farm shop. Wherever we buy, do we think about how fresh and wholesome it is. Has it travelled from half way around the world to get to the supermarkets shelves?

It has to be said that next to producing your own, local is fresher and usually tastier. I give you an example, I can go into the garden and pick runner beans, I can go into Tim's or the village shop and buy some local fresh beans, or I can buy some in the supermarket from Kenya, which would you prefer. Tim buys local, traceable Meat, the shop sells local boxes of good vegetables, and these outshine anything that can be bought in the big stores.

Buying food 'In Season', that is when it's at it's very best naturally, not forced on or held back but as said ' at it's very best' and when it should be cropping. So now we know where and when to buy the very best ingredients, so why do we buy acidic, hard and glassy tomatoes in the winter months when we know that by early summer through to Autumn we can have those beautifully ripe, tasty, thin skinned tomatoes that are a treat to eat.

As Tomatoes are at their best now, in season and in glut proportions, a simple tomato and basil soup that can be eaten hot, cold or even frozen to brighten up a cold winters day.

TOMATO AND BASIL SOUP.

1 lb. Ripe tomatoes, skinned and quartered.
1 large onion, chopped
1 large potato diced
1 pint of vegetable or chicken stock
About a dozen basil leaves, olive oil.
Salt and pepper to taste, a clove of garlic
1 tablespoon tomato puree

Sauté the veg then add toms. Add stock and seasoning. Bring all to a boil, and simmer for 30 mins. Blitz in a blender, add a swirl of cream. Garnish with parmesan croutons and snipped chives.

If you wish to freeze some don't add cream until use.

Do have a go better than tinned by far.

Enjoy it, good food need not break the bank.

Artisan cooking and processing

As I write this article, I am overwhelmed by my own and natures bounty. In the wild I have enjoyed wild field mushrooms, blackberries and hazel nuts. At home with a glut of tomatoes I have made lots of tomato soup, ketchup, pizza topping, tomato chilli jam and several baking trays of oven dried tomatoes with garlic, olive oil, thyme and sea salt and black pepper roasted on a very low heat for 3 hours, these I freeze and use when tomatoes are out of season. With windfall apples I made brown sauce (try it you will never buy H.P. again), apple wine, and not forgetting apple chutney. Most things can be made quite quickly, and very cheaply, do have a go. Last week I bought 'the first of the new season's' Cornish sprats from Don Jones's Wellington fishmongers and I hot smoked half of them and they were delicious. And to me, that's what in season is all about, enjoying something you have not tasted for a whole season.

Lamb Hot pot.
Quantity will feed six so half or cut into thirds should you require less.

12, best end of neck chops (can use scrag end for economy, but may need a little longer cooking).
1 lb. Onions thinly sliced.
2 lbs. Potatoes thinly sliced.
Salt, pepper, water or light stock butter.

In a deep casserole put the meat and veg in layers, seasoning each layer with salt and black pepper. Finish off with an overlapping layer of potatoes. Pour in enough water or stock to come 1/2 way up the pot.

Brush the top layer of potatoes with melted butter. Cover and put into a hot oven mark 6-8. 200 c. for 30 mins, then reduce heat to mark 1. 140c. and leave for 2 1/2 hours, taking off the lid after 2 hours so the potatoes can brown.

A simple 1 pot dish with bags of flavour, fit for a King.

Do have a go and enjoy.

November. Artisan cooking and processing.

By the time you read this months page I would have had tasted my first pheasant of the season, and what a treat they are. If you have not tried it ask Tim our butcher for one as they are not expensive, and plain roasted with stuffing and a few rashers of streaky bacon on top is most delicious. I have since last months article made some spiced pickled pears, cucumber, mint jelly with cider, bottled more beer (Bishop's Ale), and made some smoky red tomato chutney. I have also salted more runner beans since they came back in abundance.

This time of year is a good time to make pickles to accompany Christmas cold meats etc. and I am turning my thoughts to making a cheese for the festive season.

Apple day has passed so for me it was a time to visit Robin Small at Charlton Orchards as I usually get a box of apples and my all time favourite is an old russet called 'Orleans Reinette', and I have had my first crop this year from my very own trees. So do go along to the shop and orchards at Charlton Nr. Creech St. Michael where you can taste before you buy many varieties old and new, like 'Adams pearmain' and all those tasty ones that you won't find in supermarkets.

October sees many squashes in the farm shops and markets including Butternut squash, so as they are in season here is my recipe for a lovely winter warming soup.

BUTTERNUT AND ORANGE SOUP.

1 butternut squash, 1lb. Plus. Peeled and chopped.
Zest and juice of 1/2 Orange.
1 Apple peeled, cored and diced.
2 Onions, finely chopped.
3 Tablespoons of butter.
1/2Teaspoon curry powder, pinch nutmeg, 1 bay leaf.
750 mls. Chicken or vegetable stock.
Salt and pepper to taste.
Yoghurt or cream to garnish.

Sauté onions until tender, add squash for a further three mins.
Add all other ingredients except the garnish. Cook until tender and then liquidise. Check for seasoning and consistency.

Do have a go and enjoy.

Artisan cooking and processing.
December.

December is here and it brings into season one of my favourite vegetables, 'Brussels sprouts' which to me is Christmas dinner. December also has to be hearty, warming meals, which conjure up bowls of steaming oxtail casserole or a stew of long cooked shin of beef. In season at the moment are most of the game, crab, lobster, sprats, mussels, chestnuts, wild fungi, late apples and all sorts of good winter vegetables. What a choice we have, never mind Argentinean beetroots or Kenyan French beans as we have good quality 'in season veg'.

Christmas is when all the family come to spend time, and a Turkey, goose or whatever you prefer is a joy to share. I love to share the things I have made at this time and I put together a small box ,covered in Christmas paper and some straw into it. I put in jars of pickled onions, chutneys, a bottle of home made 'Bishop's Ale, mince pies and a pudding. This I give to good neighbours, one such neighbour has got hooked on my chilli jam, so I must see to it that he gets a jar. Having spoken about warming winter meals, I thought I would post a recipe for an Oxtail stew, yet another 1 pot dish.

Oxtail stew

1 oxtail ,cut into pieces
2 Tblsp. Olive oil
2 ozs. Fat bacon chopped
1 onion chopped
1 clove garlic chopped
8 fld. Oz. White wine
salt and pepper
1/2 Pint beef stock
2 celery sticks chopped
4 tomatoes, skinned and quartered
Chopped parsley to garnish.

Sauté bacon, onion and garlic until transparent.
Add oxtail and cook on all sides until browned.
Add wine, stock and season with salt and pepper.
Cover and braise over a gentle heat for about
2.1/2. hours, add a little more stock if required.
About 30 mins. Before the end of cooking add
the celery and about 15 mins before the end add
tomatoes and give a good stir. Taste and adjust
seasoning as necessary, Sprinkle on the chopped
parsley and serve.

I would like to take this opportunity to wish
everyone a healthy, happy and peaceful
Christmas.

Enjoy.

Roy Baker

ARTISAN
COOKING
AND
PROCESSING
2007

Artisan cooking and processing.
January 2007
Firstly I would like to wish everyone a very
happy, healthy and peaceful new year.

January for me is a good time of year for making all
kinds of air dried meats, salami's and chorizo's as there
are no flies to spoil the sausages. My recipe for artisan
salami is as follows.

800 gms. Lean pork shoulder,
200 gms. Backfat,
20 gms. Salt,
1 level teaspoon Prague powder, also know as 'Cure 2'
(this can be obtained from Franco (post free)
www.sausagemaking.org
e mail sales @ sausagemaking.org
or tel. 01204 433523
he also sells bacon cures, sausage seasonings, skins
etc.etc.)

2 cloves of garlic, crushed,
2 teaspoons of black peppercorns cracked,
200 mls. Red wine and some sausage skins.

Mince the pork coarsely and chop the fat at approx 1/2
inch dice.
Mix all well together and stuff the skins, I use ox
runners for salami, and tie with string at 6 inches leaving
a loop to hang it from.

Hang them to dry at around 60deg. for 2 days then hang outdoors, under cover in an airy position for between 4 and 10 weeks until dry with a slight 'give'.
Acidophylus can be dusted on the skin from the beginning to encourage the white mould, but I brush the mould from a shop bought salami onto the sausage and it soon grows away.

To make air dried chorizo's use the same recipe with the additions of sweet paprika, smoked paprika and a teaspoon of cayenne pepper, more if liked hotter. Fennel seeds can also be added if liked. Once dried they will last, (if you can resist) for months.
We still have good seasonal foods available, our Butcher Tim has rabbits, pheasants, venison etc. as well as his usual meat's, and Carl next door has good vegetables and I have at last tried the 'organic box scheme' and was very happy with the contents, which are soil association registered. My view is they were very fresh and tasty, as if they had just been picked from my garden. Some of the roots still have a little soil on them which to my way of thinking is a good thing, unlike supermarket veg which has been super cleaned with lord knows what and it all takes time which puts a few more days on the age.

So January is with us and it reminds me that we have started again in the growing of veg. Time to sow my onion seed, early tomatoes, peppers, chilli's, for the greenhouse. As I grow and use loads of herbs I like to grow some early parsley in modules to plant outside under cloches later. Editor Bob has asked me to increase the size of my article so I hope you will not get information overload!!! Time now for my recipe.

Beef Olives.

Serves 4
8 slices of topside or braising steak about 1/2 inch thick beaten out between two pieces of cling film until they have spread to about 5 inches.
2 Onions finely sliced,
2 tblspns oil,
2 carrots diced,
1/2 Pint beef stock,
1/2 lb. Tomatoes skinned seeded and chopped,
1 clove garlic crushed,
1 bay leaf, salt and pepper.

For the stuffing
6 oz. Minced pork and a slice of bacon, minced,
a small onion chopped finely,
1 oz. Butter,
1 oz. Fresh breadcrumbs,
1 tbsp. Fresh parsley chopped,
 a few sage leaves,
grated rind of 1 lemon,
1 egg beaten, salt and black pepper

Heat oven to gas mark 4, 180 c.

mix the stuffing ingredients seasoning as you go.

Now divide the mix between the beef, and roll keeping the edges up over the stuffing until you have a little roll like a spring roll. Use a cocktail stick to secure it.

Heat the oil in a pan and brown the olives and put into a casserole.

Add the onions and carrots to the frying pan and cook until softened. Stir in the stock, tomatoes, garlic, bay and season to taste, bring to a boil. Pour this mixture over the beef olives.

Cover the dish and cook for about 1 1/2 hours or until tender, remove cocktail sticks and serve.

Enjoy.

Artisan cooking and processing. February 2007.

February sees the end of the pheasant season, but being almost self reliant I have a nice little stock in my freezers. I do like to hang pheasants until they are quite 'gamy' (often up to three weeks in cold weather) although this winter has, so far been mild and about nine days has been long enough. Hare is still in season, and now is the best time for brown crabs, both cock and hen. Vegetables to enjoy now are Brussels sprouts, kales, leeks, Swedes, cabbages, onions, chicory, endives and Jerusalem artichokes. Talking of white cabbage, I am just about to make some sauerkraut, which is salted and fermented cabbage. It takes a couple of weeks to do and is often eaten with fresh and cured pork. My Sons Partner, Vesna is Serbian and her Mother came over for the birth of my new Grandson Thomas Alexander Baker who was born on New Years Eve and she brought me a Serbian cookbook printed in English. There are many traditional peasant and rustic dishes to have a go at. I must admit they have got it right as family is all and is at the heart of life including eating with family and talking.

I have been busy sowing seeds for my vegetable plot, so that is ongoing now and tomatoes (which is one of my favourites) are always sown in many varieties and last year I grew 28 different types, red, pink, orange, yellow, white, black, striped and green. All are old heritage varieties, which taste beautiful. I make up tomato sauce for pasta and pizza toppings, tomato ketchup and I often bottle some for the winter. Tomatoes are so easy to grow and are so prolific, and just two plants in a border will provide you with as many as you would normally want. I am not in favour of grow bags as there are problems with exact watering regimes and this can spell disaster.

February brings cold, bright weather usually and when the cold bites I think of warm comforting food and if like me you look back at your youth, then for me it has to be Steak and Kidney Pudding. Back at Bishop's Hull primary school in the 40's school dinners were dished out by Aunty Mary Drew, Mrs. King, and Mrs Stark and I well remember the Steak and Kidney pud was fabulous. We make it today through the winter so I thought I would share it with you.

Steak and Kidney Pudding.

Filling.
2 lbs beef, skirt, shin or chuck. Cubed
1 lb. Beef kidneys cored and cubed
salt and pepper
1 glass red wine, (to deglaze)
2 medium onions, sliced
2 oz. Seasoned flour, to coat meat
1 tablespoon tomato ketchup
1 teaspoon English mustard
a bay leaf and about 1.1/4. pints stock

8 ozs, button mushrooms, optional.

Suet crust.
1 lb. Self raising flour.
8 oz. Suet, shredded
pinch of salt
Water.

Into a hot pan put some oil, the meat that has
been tossed in the seasoned flour and brown.
When all has browned deglaze the empty pan
with the wine and add the deglazed juices into the
pan with the meat.
Now in a clean pan sweat the onions until
softened.
Add to the meat with the ketchup, mustard and
bay leaf and stock.
Stir gently and bring to a tremulous simmer.
Cook for about one and a half hours and check
seasoning at the end and adjust if necessary.
If you like mushrooms in your pudding, fry them
and add now.
Make the suet crust. Put flour into a bowl, add
pinch of salt and cold water until you have a
firmish dough. Put aside one-third for a lid. Roll
out the rest and line a 3-pint size basin.
Pile in the meat and it's gravy. Now roll out the
lid and wet the edges and press it onto the top of
the pudding.
Fold and a double layer of grease proof paper
with a pleat in, now tie on a cloth or muslin and
fashion a handle with the string. Place in a

steamer or improvise with an upturned saucer inside a saucepan of water that comes one-third up the basin. Steam for 2 hours or longer, it wont hurt the pud.

 Turn out the pudding and serve with buttery mashed potatoes and Kale.

 This should feed 4-6 people so halve it or you may pop.

Enjoy.

Artisan cooking and processing March

March is a time to look forward to spring when we can perhaps leave some of the winter roots behind and look forward to fresh spring vegetables, like purple sprouting broccoli, spring cabbage, saladines, seakale and cauliflower etc. The wild larder too is providing more and more leafy greens as the weather warms the soil like Alexanders, chickweed, chives, wild chervil (cow parsley), fat hen, nettles and watercress. Hare is still in season but not so readily available. Now the new seasons rhubarb is a real treat with those long pink forced stems.

Nettles and blue cheese is a good filling for ravioli. First make your pasta, I use pasta flour, ie. 10 ozs. Flour, three eggs, 1/2 teaspoon salt, 1 dessertspoon olive oil, mix together and work well until a stiffish dough is obtained, leave in the fridge to relax for 30 mins.

In the meantime, wash the nettles use young tops. Put in a pan of boiling water with a pinch or two of salt and cook until tender. Refresh in cold water, squeeze the water out and chop. Now roll out the pasta either with a rolling pin or a pasta mill quite thinly. With a round scone cutter cut circles out of the pasta. Now crumble some blue cheese into the nettles, you can use Gorgonzola, Stilton, whatever. Mix together and place a teaspoon full into the centre of half of the circles, wet the edges with a pastry brush and put a plain circle on top and seal the edges. Cook in boiling salted water for approx 6 mins. Knapp with tomato sauce or olive oil and pesto. A sprinkle of grated Parmesan is good.

Referring to the glut of tomatoes I was talking about last month, I have decided to buy from seeds of Italy a ''passa Pomodori'' (a tomato press), which makes passata from tomatoes at the rate of 50 kilos in an hour. It's cranked a hand press as I am a bit of a luddite as well as an artisan. My onions and garlic are growing apace now and the tomatoes are pricked off so tomato sauce, here we come. Many vegetables can be grown in containers which is more convenient for some of us as you can grow a few of this and that. A few runner beans in a tub will produce a fine crop of beans, as long as you pick regularly and water well. Let's all grow a vegetable this year in a tub, large pot or border and when we harvest it we can taste for ourselves how fresh and tasty 'real food' is.

For anyone interested in wine making March is the time to tap some sap from the silver birch tree to make a delicious birch sap wine. Done properly it does not harm the tree at all.

I haven't as yet given a fish recipe so I will start with an all time favourite Fish Pie.

Fish pie.

1 1/2 lbs Mixed fish, example smoked haddock, salmon, cod.
1 pint fish, chicken or veg stock and milk mixed
1-2 hard-boiled eggs chopped.
1 1/2 ozs. Butter.
1 oz, flour.
Salt and black pepper.
A good tablespoon chopped parsley and capers.
1/2 lb boiled potatoes, mashed with butter and milk.

Poach fish in the stock and milk for 5-6 mins. Drain reserving the stock.
Skin and debone fish and break into pieces, put into the pie dish and add the eggs.
Make a rue with the flour and butter, pour on the hot stock and milk, stirring all the time, season and stir in the parsley and capers and pour over the fish.
Cover with the mashed potato and cook in a hot oven 190 degrees, gas mark 5. for 25 mins.
Raise the heat for the last few minuets or put under a grill to brown.

Enjoy.

Artisan cooking and processing April.

Seasonal foods to enjoy in April are purple
sprouting, spring
Cabbages, cauliflowers, lettuce, seakale, sorrel and
watercress. There are now a few wild mushrooms to
be sought out and morels and St. George's
mushrooms are a rare treat if you can find them. I
have found morels, not in the woods but growing on
shrub beds that have been mulched with bark
chippings. Very expensive to buy either fresh or
dried which makes them all the more delectable
when you pick a kilo or two. There are also nice wild
greens to be had, Alexander's, chives, chickweed, fat
hen, hogweed shoots, wild garlic, dandelions,
watercress, hop shoots, (as good as asparagus),
meadow sweet, seakale, sea spinach and wild rocket
leaves. Also in season, crab, Pollack, sea trout, wood
pigeon and forced and outdoor rhubarb.
In April I have my first cutting of asparagus spears
which when freshly cut and in the pan within
minuets is so very different to bought in spears that
have been hanging around in a supermarket, as it is
so much more sweet.
On the 14th. Of this month I sow my runner beans in
pots in a cold greenhouse, and then I can start to pick
beans the first week of July and right through until
the end of October.
I salted some last year and have several pounds left.
I use 3 lbs. Prepared beans to 1lb. Salt and it makes
it's own brine. It is time too for planting out onions
grown from seed back in January. I have also sown

parsley and chervil in quantity as I cannot cook without herbs. I am currently planting tomatoes in the cold greenhouse, they have come to flower and will be producing those long awaited tomatoes quite soon.

Easter time is here and I usually make hot cross buns and Easter biscuits. It is a tradition to make a simnel cake and primrose flower heads (which are edible) one for each of the disciples to decorate the top. Good Friday was always in our family a time for salt cod for dinner and I haven't had that for a number of years so I may well try to find some as it also makes a wonderful dish, pulverised with olive oil, garlic, and potato called 'Brandade' which is baked in the oven until browned slightly and served on toast. I wonder how many of us make our own bread, a daily staple but when we get into making it there is so many tastes and flavours to enjoy, and I often make cheese and tomato breads, cheese and herb with garlic. I have also made up a recipe for one of my grandsons to make a chocolate bread on which he spreads 'nutella'.

Steak with stout

1lb. Stewing steak
2 oz. Butter
2 onions sliced
thyme, sage, parsley and bay leaf.
4 fld.oz. stout
8 fl. oz. Beef stock
salt and pepper.

3 potatoes
roux to thicken, optional
chopped parsley

Brown the meat in half butter, add the onions and
cook for 3 mins, add herbs, tied together, pour over
the stout and stock and season to taste.
Top with the whole peeled potatoes, cover tightly
and simmer gently for 2 hours until ready.
The juices may be slightly thickened with a roux
and enriched with the remaining butter.
Serve the meat surrounded by the potatoes and
sprinkled with chopped parsley.

Enjoy.

Artisan Cooking and processing, May.

May is neither summer nor spring it is for me a transitional time when we are not enjoying the luxurious summer vegetables and fruit yet but the spring foods are few and far between now. I am still enjoying asparagus and with some of my quail eggs make a very nice tartlet.

Foods in season now are asparagus, cabbages, carrots, cauliflower, lettuce, radish, rocket, seakale, sorrel, watercress, rhubarb, wild garlic, dandelions, hogweed shoots, hop shoots, meadow sweet leaves, St.George's mushrooms, morels, and pig nuts.

In the garden I am planting out runner beans, (I can't do without them) and at the end of the month outdoor tomatoes can be planted, along with peppers, chillies, aubergines, cucumbers, courgettes, and pumpkins. It's a time to look ahead to hopefully a great harvest. We know we can do so much with our veg and fruit. I have utilised some of our fencing panels to grow some top fruit against, and to date I have 6 apple trees, 1 plum, 2 pear, 2 figs, 2 grapes, and 1 olive, not to mention raspberry canes, loganberry, blackberry, 2 blueberries, strawberries, rhubarb and a hazel nut. I am trying a few melons again this year.

I must make some more cheese again as that too is well worth the effort and not at all hard to do. I made some of the bits and bobs required. My mould is a 4.1/2. inch x 6 inch plastic drainpipe with small holes drilled into the sides (to let the whey out), aboard to stand on (ply), a cheese mat, plastic mesh and a follower which is a piece of wood turned by a friend on his lathe to fit the inside of the drainpipe (mould).

To make the cheese I bring a gallon of milk to 85 degrees F. and maintain this temperature whilst I add a starter (small pot of natural yoghurt). Maintain temperature for about 40 mins. Now add rennet as per instructions and stir well, maintain temperature for another 40 mins. Now test that the curd has set so you can cut your curd vertically and horizontally and leave for 30 mins lightly stirring a couple of times at the same time raising the temperature to 100deg.F. Next drain the curds through a cheesecloth and colander. Leave the curds to drain overnight in the cheesecloth. Next morning add around 1 oz. Salt and mix well, breaking up the curds as you go. Now place your mould on the board and push the curds into the mould and press down with your follower and place some weights on top. Turn your cheese over daily for 3 days by taking off the follower, place a board on top then invert the mould. Now place follower on top. After 3 days remove your cheese by placing it on a clean board and push down on the follower until the cheese slides out.

Leave it to dry off for a day then paint on some lard that has been melted. This will protect the cheese and keep air out. For a few weeks you need to turn the cheese over every 2 days. If you can resist it no longer, then try it now it will be the best. If you can leave it for another week or two it will be even better.

Now to continue my one pot meals I give you

Poule au Pot

1 Large boiling fowl
6 carrots
3 turnips
3 leeks
1 celery heart
1 med. Onion
3 whole cloves
salt and pepper.
Bouquet garni of thyme, bay leaf and parsley.

Wash veg, tie leeks in a bundle and herbs.
Spike the onion with cloves.
Place chicken in a large saucepan, cover with water
and bring to a boil, skimming when necessary.
Season with salt and pepper add vegetables and herbs.
Simmer for 2 hours then remove the chicken and
carve, serve surrounded by the vegetables.
The gravy is served separately as a broth.

Do try it, as it feeds a few hungry people.

Enjoy.

Artisan cooking and processing June

We are now into summer and we are talking
strawberries, cherries, gooseberries, and
raspberries. In the vegetable plot we still have
asparagus, broad beans, carrots, cauliflower,
lettuce, peas, radish, rocket and watercress.
Elderflowers are in blossom and as well as wine,
lemonade etc. we dip the flowering heads into
batter and deep fry until golden then drizzle on
some honey, lovely.

All manner of fish and shellfish are in season
now, mainly black bream, spider crab, signal
crayfish, cuttlefish, mackerel, Pollack, wild
salmon, sea bass, trout and sea trout.

In the wild, pig nuts, St.George's mushroom,
horseradish and sea spinach are there for the
taking.

I am currently planting, for the winter, greens
like kales, more Brussels sprouts, and broccoli.
You always look ahead to the next season when
growing for the table. My garlic is nearly ready to
harvest and it is looking good. I am too growing
an Italian green, which is called 'cima di rapa'
and is a quick maturing turnip top/flowering
shoot and is a little bit bitter like a kale except it
is grown in the summer. All the fruit is looking
good and I must remember to net the cherries,
strawberries and raspberries etc.

The whole point of growing veg. Etc is that
you can get to know the best varieties that suit
your personal tastes. If our vegetables and fruit

comes from the supermarket we have to buy what they consider best, i.e. Long shelf life and under ripe most often.

My tomatoes are ripening and I am looking forward to a real tomato again. I have been, and still am cutting lettuce from mid April to date.

The weather in June usually allows us outdoor eating and bar-b-qs. It is nice to have friends or family around you and sharing some food cooked outdoors. I often make sausages and some I smoke on a little hot smoker I have. Mackerel or trout is good smoked as well and it's a handy variation to a Barbie. It is so easy to make some burgers either lamb, beef, or pork as you can add mint, apple etc. and they are going to taste so much better. I'm afraid I make my own relishes as well to go with them like tomato chilli jam, smoked red pepper chutney, brown sauce and tomato ketchup. You will also need some bread rolls and they take no time to make. Then out into the garden for some vegetable kebabs. Cherry tomatoes, peppers, courgettes and onions. Tim's lamb kebabs are nice and you don't have to make it all yourself. A few sticky ribs and some homemade ale or wine and you have quite a feast. I have been known to make 'Bunny burgers and bunny bangers' and very nice they are too.

In June the mackerel is in season and just plain fried or grilled with that other seasonal fruit the gooseberry, made into a sauce by just taking 1/2 lb. Gooseberries, knob of butter in a pan and cook away until soft, mashing with a fork, then stir in 1/2 pint of double cream and a touch of sugar. That's a very seasonal, and easy but delicious meal.

It's time for my recipe and as new seasons lamb is here I will break from old habits and leave you with an Indian dish, so do try it.

LAMB BIRYANI (a mild rice dish)

6 oz. Basmati rice
25 fl oz. Water
1 small onion, finely chopped
1 green chilli, finely chopped
8 oz. Lamb cut into 1/2 inch cubes
1/2 Teaspoon turmeric
1 teaspoon salt
1/2 Teaspoon chilli powder
2 teaspoons soy sauce
3 oz. Frozen peas
3 oz. Carrots diced small

Wash the rice. Into a large pan mix the water, onion, green chilli, lamb, turmeric, salt, chilli powder and soy sauce. Bring to the boil, cover the pan, reduce the heat and let the mixture simmer for about 35 minutes. Add washed rice, peas and carrots, bring back to the boil then reduce heat again. Cover the pan and simmer gently for about 12 mins. The rice should look dry. Serve with a vegetable dish or with Dhal.

Enjoy the seasons.

Artisan processing and cooking July.

July brings forth a rich harvest of seasonal foods.
We have globe artichokes, beetroot, broad beans,
carrots, cauliflower, courgette, French beans,
runner beans, garlic, kohlrabi, lambs lettuce,
onions, pakchoy, peas, potatoes, perslane, radish,
rocket, samphire, sorrel, spinach, tomatoes and
watercress.
 Apricots, black, red and white currants,
blueberries, gooseberries, strawberries,
raspberries, cherries and rhubarb.
 In the wild there is horseradish, marsh samphire,
elderflower, wild strawberries, chanterelles,
chicken of the woods fungi, pignuts, rabbit,
woodpigeon, crab, crayfish, cuttlefish, lobster,
trout, scallops, sea bass and mackerel.
 With all that choice we really have a rich and
bountiful table of food to enjoy and celebrate. By
the time you read this I would have tasted my
first tomato of the season and my first runner
beans. It's always a treat and a pleasure to pick
and eat the first of the new season.
 I was privileged to be given a rather large trout
from Fred Yeandle and I had to do it justice so I
took off the two fillets, deboned them and 'cured'
one as smoked trout and the other half as a
gravadlax, so both were cured and not cooked.
One is salt and sugar and smoke and the other is
sugar, salt, mustard, lime zest and juice with lots
of home grown dill weed. Well they both tasted
fantastic with a salad of mixed lettuce and rocket

with orange segments. Thanks again Fred they were so good. Bishop's Hull produces some truly great and generous people.

A very good friend that I 'met' on the Internet and have since met several times keeps old variety pigs lambs, turkeys, ducks and chickens in their woods in Lynton North Devon. Some of their pigs are Gloster old spots, Berkshires, Tamworths and Wild boar crosses. A few weeks ago she sent me two pigs heads, some hocks and some loin which was a bit fatty, this was from her wild boar crossed Tamworth as she wanted me to taste the meat. Well I made five basins of brawn, crispy pigs ears, lots of pork and leek and pork and herb sausages and some sweet, dry cured bacon and smoked dry cured bacon. It was a truly wonderful batch of bacon and sausages. Having given a couple of brawns away, I was told that I was (this time) a bit short on seasonings. Well you have to have quality control some how. I was obviously not focussed or having a senior moment.

Now to my recipe.
I love this one for a quick and tasty meal.

Beef Stroganoff. Serves 3.

12 oz. Fillet steak sliced thinly in 2 inch pieces
salt and fresh ground pepper.
2 teaspoons flour.

1 oz. Butter.
1 medium onion finely sliced into rings.
4 oz. Button mushrooms finely sliced.
About 1 eighth of a Pint soured cream.
Hot boiled rice to serve.

Season steak with salt and pepper and toss in flour. Melt half the butter in a frying pan, add the onion rings and fry until just coloured and remove to a plate.

Fry the mushrooms for a few minuets adding more butter if necessary. Remove the mushrooms to the onion plate, add remaining butter to the pan and when hot put in the beef strips and fry briskly for 3-4 mins. Return the onions and mushrooms to the pan with plenty of salt and pepper, shake over heat for 1 minute. Add soured cream to the pan and cook until heated through.

Serve with boiled rice, noodles or, if liked crisp fried matchstick potatoes.

Note: A less expensive version of beef stroganoff is made with flank steak, which takes very well to this light cooking. Should be cut across the grain.

I hope you enjoy this one as much as me.

Enjoy.

Artisan cooking and processing, August.

August for me means gluts of vegetables.
Tomatoes and runner beans are given away to
neighbours and family, as are cucumbers,
courgettes, and salads. There is so much in
season now. We have some early apples,
Discovery, George cave, Redsleeves, plums,
gages, raspberries, etc. With vegetables there are
globe artichokes, aubergines, beetroot, carrots,
cauli, cabbage, chard, cucumber, fennel, kohl
rabi, onion, pak choy, peas, runner beans, French
beans, watercress, spinach, sweetcorn, tomatoes,
peppers, chillis, and so on. In the wild larder
there is samphire, horseradish, blackberries,
whortleberries, wild strawberries, ceps,
chanterelles, chicken of the woods, field
mushroom, horse mushrooms, parasols, giant
puffballs, rabbit, wood pigeon, trout, squid, sea
bass, mackerel, Pollack, scallops, lobster, brown
and spider crab and fresh water crayfish. Now is
certainly the time to try some wild food.
 There have been times when as a newly married
man I have gone out into the countryside, early in
the morning and came home with horse
mushrooms the size of dinner plates, hazel nuts,
watercress picked from a small stream,
blackberries, giant puffballs etc. On other
occasions I went fishing in the Tone and returned
with perch, eels and on a few occasions, fishing
below the weir at Knapp, I have caught a few

nice plaice, yes plaice, you could have knocked me down with a feather.

It has been a little quiet this month so I will go straight on to my recipe. I am running out of my brown sauce which is better than HP or Ok. And I more importantly know what is in it, so here it is.

2lbs. Cooking apples diced
1/2 Lb. Prunes
1 large onion chopped
1.1/2. pints of malt vinegar.
1 teaspoon ground ginger
1/2 Tspn. Ground nutmeg
1/2 Tspn. Cayenne pepper
1/2 Tspn. Allspice
1/2 Cup table salt
1 lb. Brown sugar.
3-4 jars or bottles sterilised.

Put all the fruit into a pot of water and cook until tender. Strain and push through a sieve. Add vinegar, spices, salt and sugar and cook on low heat until thick. Pour into sterilised sauce bottles or jars, and if you want it to keep for a couple of years then it should be sterilised in a water bath at 100degrees for 20 mins then screw down the caps. The last couple of times I have made it I didn't bother to sterilise and it kept for 1 year ok. It never last's that long as the family all like it and share it with me.!!!

Artisan cooking and processing. September.

In September we have a multitude of seasonal fruit, vegetables, fungi, fish and game. There is globe artichokes, aubergines, beetroots, borlotti beans (for podding), broccoli, cabbage, carrots, cauliflower, chard, courgettes, cucumber, fennel, garlic, kale, kohl rabi, lambs lettuce, onions, pak choy, peppers, chillis, pumpkins, rocket, runner beans, salsify, scorzonera, sorrel, spinach, sweetcorn, tomatoes and watercress.

With the fruit we have early apples, discovery, George Cave, and red sleeves, late Egremont russet, Blenheim Orange, and Orleans Reinette. Blackberries, blueberries, damsons, greengages, peaches and nectarines, early and mid season pears, Beth, Williams and Merton pride. Plums, lots of fungi in the wild, ceps, chanterelles, chicken of the woods, field mushrooms, horse mushrooms, oyster mushrooms, parasols, giant puffballs and shaggy ink caps. Plenty of fish, crab, eels, lobster, mussels, oyster, mackerel, scallops, sea bass, sprats, squid and river trout.

There is some game in season too, grey squirrel, grouse, mallard, rabbit and wood pigeon. With seasonal foods in such abundance why do we need Australian Brussels sprouts and shallots? I have had a glut of runner beans so I have given them away to family and neighbours and they do appreciate the 'home grown taste'.

I have mentioned before that I make my own
sausages so to that end I have sent off to buy a
sausage stuffer. I have to date used a Kenwood
chef with mincing attachment and sausage
nozzles but the sausage meat goes down a bit too
fine and I want to make courser ones like
Toulouse which use chopped meat instead of
minced, this will be better for salami and chorizo
too.

It is at this time of the year that I like to go into
the woods and look for Ceps or Penny Buns
(boletus edulis), Hedgehog mushrooms (Hydnum
repandum), Parasols (lepiota procera), Shaggy
ink caps (coprinus comatus), and Wood blewits
(Lepista nuda) and Chicken of the wood
(laetisporus sulphurous). Just chopped and fried
in butter with parsley added with perhaps a
chopped clove of garlic is worth waiting a whole
year for. I have frozen ceps/penny buns and they
do hold their shape and taste very well. When
you go out foraging for wild mushrooms you
really MUST Know what you are looking for
and never eat anything you cannot positively
identify. The nature conservancy council run
'Fungus forays' usually October November time
and these are advertised in the library. I have
been on a few and identifying, cooking and
tasting them knowing the leader of the foray
knows exactly what is edible is a satisfying day
out. They are often arranged for Fyne Court.

All this talk of tasty mushrooms has got me thinking food, so here is a tasty mushroom soup known as witches brew.

Witches Brew. Serves 4.

8 oz. Mixed mushrooms (when you come home with a couple of these and a few of those and so on.).
2 tablespoons butter
1 small onion peeled and sliced.
1 oz. Sweet cured bacon. Cut into strips.
1 small cooked potato, mashed.
1 1/2 Pints of beef or chicken stock.
1 small carton single cream.
2 tablespoons sour cream.
2 egg yolks
2 tablespoons finely chopped chives.
Salt and black pepper to taste.

Cut larger mushrooms into chunks but leave the smaller ones whole.
Fry the onion in the butter, and after a few minuets add the bacon and continue frying.
Now add the mashed potato, stir in well and fry a little longer.
Turn the mixture into a saucepan, add stock, stirring well, bring to a boil and simmer until everything is well cooked.
Remove from heat, stir in the cream, sour cream, beaten egg yolks and season to taste.

Return to heat, add chives stir in and serve with home made wholemeal bread and butter.

Enjoy.

ARTISAN COOKING AND PROCESSING
OCTOBER.

Nature now spreads around in dreamy hue
A pall to cover all that summer knew.

October <u>is</u> autumn and the seasons foods show it
well. Squashes and pumpkins, Jerusalem
artichokes, Brussels sprouts, red cabbage, celery,
parsnips, chicory, apples, chestnuts, crab apples,
damsons and bullaces, medlar, quince,
blackberries, walnuts, rabbit, hare, mallard,
partridge, grouse, pheasant, squirrel, woodcock,
wood pigeon, eels, oysters, brown and spider
crabs, elderberries, rose hips, rowan berries,
sloes, chanterelles, hedgehog fungus, oyster,
giant puffball, shaggy ink caps, wood blewits,
and one of my favourites, parasols. In fact there
is lots to enjoy before the winter descends upon
us.
 Now is a good time to preserve some of your
surplus vegetables and fruit for the Christmas
festivities. I usually pickle some onions or
shallots, sweet pickled cauliflower, sliced
cucumbers, spiced pickled pears and mixed
pickles not to leave out some piccalilli.
 To date I have used my 'pomadoro' (tomato
press) and it made passata from a trug full of
Italian 'San Marzano' tomatoes in no time. I am
very impressed with it. I have also christened my
sausage stuffing machine and made 10 lbs. Of
sausages in four varieties, Italian pork with sun

dried tomatoes, fennel seeds, basil and pine nuts, pork and leek, sage and spices and garlic and herb. I was given some windfall apples so I made 10 bottles of my brown sauce (recipe last month which went very well with the Cornish pasties I made.

In the garden and greenhouses I still have tomatoes, peppers, chillies, and also have a few beans, cabbage, beetroots, and my Brussels are almost ready to start picking. Years ago I used to grow a red variety called Rubine, it was quite small and I would pickle some for Christmas. I have sown some more lettuce for Christmas and the New Year together with some over wintering 'spring onions'. Time now too for planting some garlic for next June harvest. I can never grow enough and the same goes for herbs. I have some parsley which I sowed to take me through the winter months as covered with a cloche will give it enough protection.

As autumn closes in I think of warming casseroles and stews like oxtail, rabbit and I like lamb too and if it is cooked one day and left to cool and eaten the next day then the fat (and you will get an amount) can easily be taken off when it is cold and set. A nice stew with a few dumplings made from flour, breadcrumbs, suet, parsley, and grated lemon zest, salt and pepper makes a nice light dumpling with a fresh lemony flavour that will lift the stew. Now I am talking food I am thinking recipes so onward to my recipe for this month.

PORK AND APPLE SAVOURY

4 pork chops or cutlets
4 Desert apples.
4 large potatoes.
4 small onions.
1/2 Pint stock.
Salt, pepper and sage leaves.

 Sprinkle your chops with the salt, pepper and
chopped sage leaves. Place them in a large
ovenproof casserole. Peel and slice onions and
apples and put in layers seasoning as you go on
top of the chops. Pour on the stock. Peel and slice
the potatoes very thinly and layer over the apples
and onions, making a circular pattern. Cover and
cook in a moderate oven 180c. gas mark 4 for
1.1/2. to 2 Hours. Yet another 1 pot complete
meal.

Enjoy your food.

Artisan cooking and processing, November

NO LEAVES, NO BIRDS, NOVEMBER

Seasonal foods now available are artichokes,
beetroots, Brussels sprouts, cabbage, celeriac,
carrots, celery, chard, chicory, endives, parsnips,
potatoes, pumpkins, salsify, Swede and turnip.
Fruit abounds now and do try to find some good
apples like Egremont russet, Blenheim Orange,
Ashmeads Kernel, or Orleans Reinette. Pears too
Concorde, Doyenne du Comice, Conference and
Winter Nellis. There are still to be had chestnuts,
walnuts, horse mushrooms, hedgehog fungus,
wood blewits and oyster mushrooms. Game in
season Wild goose, grouse, hare, mallard,
partridge, rabbit, snipe, woodcock, wood pigeon
and my favourite, pheasant. Sprats, squid, crab,
whiting, mackerel, lobsters, mussels, scallops and
cod.

I have now picked in my small crop of apples, I
have Holstein Cox and Orleans Reinette all
squirreled away for Christmas, they are lovely
with stilton and port. And talking of Christmas
Tim the butcher takes orders for turkey and geese
now so I must order mine. You can rely on
having good poultry from him. At last the runner
beans are over and out, it is with sadness always
as they are my all time favourite veg, (I can still
enjoy some salted ones) but a new season opens
as one closes and sprouts and kale are there for

135

me to enjoy now. I have two plantings of each so I get a follow on crop. My wife has made the Christmas puddings and mincemeat and as usual one for our neighbour.

I have made some pickled onions, sweet pickled cauliflower, beetroots and spiced pickled pears, as these all make a good accompaniment to cold meats and cheeses etc. As all my family will be with us this Christmas I will make a raised game pie which always goes down well. As I make my own recipe mini chipolatas wrapped in home dry cured bacon as a garnish for the turkey I can do this in advance and freeze them together with the two stuffings, sage and onion and chestnut.

I have made and stored some of my Bishop's Ale so we don't go dry.

It may be worth mentioning some of the kit that helps me in the processing of these Artisan foods I am so fond of. Firstly I have an old Kenwood Chef, bought in a charity shop many years ago, mincing attachment also from charity shop. I am the proud owner of an electric slicer (for my bacon etc.), I have a purpose built sausage stuffer and tomato press (pomadoro), pasta machine, mandolin, ricer, mouli, most important is some very good knives, a meat cleaver and saw for bones.

Wine corkers, filter, crown capper for beer bottles, mezaluna, cheese moulds, mats, cloths and so on.

I have also a store of many salts and cures for preserving and made up ready to use seasonings for sausages, black and white puddings, Dry and smoked bacon cures, sweet bacon cure, fish cures, etc.etc.etc. A hot smoker. a bar-b-cue, and a chiminea which cooks a mean joint. I had an e, mail from Bob this morning spurring me on, so to my recipe for November.

Game Pie cold.

A selection of game, a rabbit a pheasant, a couple of pigeons left whole, a piece of venison or whatever you can get, jointed.
1/2 lb streaky bacon cut into large dice,
1 pigs trotter,
a glass of red wine,
stock veg ie. 2 carrots, 2 onions , 2 sticks of celery, roughly chopped.
A bay leaf, sprig of thyme, plus the carcasses from the game.

Fry veg until brown, and put into pot, brown game and add to the pot together with the trotter. Add enough water to cover, bring to a boil and simmer at a slow tremble for about 1 1/2 hours. When cool, remove the meats from the bones, take bacon and any of the trotter meat off. Meanwhile continue to cook all the bone, veg and stock together to reduce what will be the jelly for your pie then strain.

Roll out some rough puff pastry and line a suitable tin.

Add the game meat, bacon and trotter meat, add some of the reduced stock to just below the meat, make a pastry lid with a small hole in the top place on top of the pie.

Decorate with pastry leaves etc. and brush with egg wash.

Bake at gas mark 5, or 190.c. for about 50 mins to 1 hour.

Serve when cold and the jelly has set, with pickles and salad.

An ideal Christmas supper.

Enjoy.

Artisan Cooking and Processing, December.

December can be quite frugal in seasonal foods we are needing hot comforting foods and that's what is available now. Our vegetables consist of Jerusalem artichokes, Brussels sprouts and tops, red cabbage, white and green, carrot, celeriac, celery, endives, kales, leeks, lettuce, onion, parsnips, potato, swede, and turnip. With the fruit we have available late apples, Egremont russet, Blenheim Orange, Orleans Reinette and in store, Cox, Fiesta, Ashmeads Kernel and bramley, forced rhubarb and chestnuts. Game available, goose, wild and farmed, grey squirrel, grouse, hare, mallard, partridge, pheasant, snipe, woodcock, and wood pigeon. Fish and shellfish, cod, crab, mussels oyster, sea bass and whiting. In the garden there are still sprouts and kales to enjoy and I have a few lettuce in the frame. I have too planted out more lettuce for the turn of the year, I have beetroots, onions, in store and salted runner beans, frozen broad beans and tomato sauces frozen. I also made from the last remnants some ratatouille using up the surplus peppers, tomatoes, courgettes, onions and garlic. I have ordered my Christmas turkey at Tim's and made chestnut stuffing and frozen that. I do tend to go overboard at Christmas but when you know the food is appreciated by the family it is all worthwhile. Last year I mulled a bottle of my Elderberry wine and it was so nice, I had to do another. As I write this (October 26th) I have just

139

made a warming rabbit stew, the first of the new season and it smells very good. I have cooked it in some boiled bacon stock so I look forward to eating that. Tim will surely have some rabbits now and they are a tasty bargain of true wild meat. I love Delia Smith's Old English rabbit pudding and make it often, it's a steamed pudding with rabbit, prunes, nutmeg and so on, a lovely pud.

I have a small purpose built hot smoker as I love smoked foods. Small whole fish like trout, mackerel, sprats, sausages, mushrooms, even boiled eggs which are nice smoked then pickled. You can improvise and easily 'make' a hot smoker from a large tin similar to the old biscuit tin or a sweet tin. Just pop a wire rack on the bottom and puncture a few holes in the sides, place the tin on a couple of bricks to create a space underneath. Now under the tin (smoker) you need a small metal container that will hold 1/2 Cup of Methelated spirits. So you are now ready to rock and roll. Put a handful of sawdust or chippings (not from treated timber or pine) ideally fruit wood or oak, etc. inside your tin, place the rack over it, place the mackerel fillet or whatever on the rack, put on the lid and light the meths and wait until the flames die out (approx 20 mins). Open the lid and hey presto 'Smoked Mackerel'. You can salt the fish for 30 mins. first to good effect but your mackerel is now ready to eat. It is time for my monthly recipe and it's another one pot dish

CHEESE AND CABBAGE CASSEROLE.

A winter meal for four

1 savoy cabbage
6 oz. Streaky bacon
2 medium cooking apples
1 large onion thinly sliced
2 Tablespoons wholemeal flour
1/2 Pint stock
6 chopped sage leaves
8 oz. Grated cheddar cheese
Heat the oven to reg. 6 or 200c.

Finely shred cabbage and cut bacon into small dice.

Peel, core and thinly slice apples.

Put bacon into large casserole and set on a low heat. When fat begins to run mix in the onion. Cook until onion is soft.

Mix in cabbage and flour, pour in the stock and bring to boil.

Mix in sage leaves and two thirds of the cheese. Cover the casserole and put into the oven for 30 mins.

Remove the lid and scatter the remaining cheese over the top of the cabbage. Put back into the oven for a further 15 mins, for the cheese to melt and begin to brown.

Serve straight from the dish.

Enjoy
Have a very happy, healthy and peaceful Christmas.

Roy Baker

WAFFLINGS
OF
A
VILLAGER

2008

Wafflings of a villager
February 2008.

I have written on artisan foods and seasonality
for a full year now and cannot repeat myself as
seasonal food is the same this February as it was
last. Bob likes me to keep up the articles and give
a monthly recipe but looking back I did a year as
'A month in our village' then on to a year
'Ramblings of a villager' and finally a year with
'Artisan cooking and processing'.

I am a devotee of all things natural, free range
and as local as possible. Hugh Fearnley
Whittingstall is running a campaign for free
range chicken called 'Chicken out', and I support
that. I am a moderator on Hugh's River Cottage
forum so I do get a lot of information from small
producers and smallholders who are pushing
ahead with fantastic tasting pork, lamb and beef
not to mention top quality poultry. There is a
growing movement towards fresh foods from
scratch and back to 'proper' cooking and I
encourage people to have a go all the time. We
have a website where recipes are posted and
anyone can take them and use - in fact, a lad on
the forum wanted to make faggots, so he googled
Faggots and he posted that my recipe came up
with my user name.
 By the time you read this, my first tomatoes will
be germinated along with peppers, aubergines,
peppers and chillies. I am still using last year's

144

chillies also my kale and Brussels have been very good this year and have been eating them since early October. There is so much I like to grow and there is never enough room for it all, but I do pack it in.

Back in December I talked about smoking foods and told how to make a smoker, well just to mention that I smoked a pheasant crown and from that with a little bacon, cream, seasonings, brandy and butter made a truly beautiful smoked pheasant pate which soon got eaten over the Christmas along with a coarse pork terrine, spiced pickled beef, jellied ox tongue and a ham. One of the few things I buy ready done is frozen flaky pastry and I use that to make Palmiers which is a sort of pastry biscuit filled with Parma ham and parmesan cheese or anchovy, parmesan and cheddar.

I will carry on with a recipe but might throw in some oriental and other foreign dishes as I do like to cook Thai, Chinese, Indian and most of all Japanese Sushi.

For my recipe this month I leave you with a lovely savoury pie, best served hot with the cheese soft and melted.

Bacon, Stilton and Cheddar Pie.

8 oz. Wholemeal shortcrust pastry seasoned with black pepper.
4 oz. Streaky bacon, diced.
1/2 oz butter.
2 medium onions finely chopped.
3 large sticks celery finely chopped.
4 oz. Stilton cheese, grated
4 oz. Farmhouse Cheddar grated.
1 tablespoon chopped fresh thyme.
4 fresh sage leaves chopped.
Beaten egg for the glaze.

Heat the oven to 200c.   gas mark 6.

Melt the butter in a pan on a low heat and add bacon, celery and onions and slowly cook until soft with no colour. Take from the heat and allow to cool.
Mix the grated cheeses in with the bacon, onions and celery together with the herbs.
Line an 8 inch flan tin with two thirds of the pastry and fill it with the filling, roll out the lid and top the pie sealing the edges.
Glaze with the beaten egg and bake for 35 mins.

Serve hot.

Enjoy.

Wafflings of a villager
March

*March comes in like a lion
and goes out like a lamb.*

Well how quickly the year seems to be going, it seems like only yesterday we were talking of Christmas.

This is a very busy time of year in the garden as there is sowing and planting to be done and talking of which, now is a good time to be sowing a half dozen French beans to an eight inch pot for some early crops that can stand under cover and give a good crop of beans without having to dig ground etc. Its an easy way to grow a few vegetables. So many vegetables can be grown on a patio in containers, a few new potatoes in an old compost bag of soil, a few runner beans in a tub or box. Salads too are easy to sow in a window box and far outshine any you could buy. It is a good time to sow a few outdoor tomatoes now to crop outside later when all fear of frost is past.

On Mothering Sunday above all other Every child should dine with It's Mother.

I was thinking of how Bishop's Hull has changed over my lifetime and expanded. We still thankfully are well off for amenities and structure in village life as we have our Church, Pub, Club,

147

Butchers, Post Office and store, Community Hall, Village Church Hall, Frank Bond Centre with all it's activities and expert tuition in all sorts of areas and now Breakfast's, We have our Good Companions, W.I., Flower Show, Cricket teams, Art Groups, Car boot sales, bingo and so on. We really must use <u>ALL</u> of these activities and services to ensure Village life (as we know it) continues.

A farmer's toast.

Let the wealthy and great
Roll in splendour and state
I envy them not I declare it
I eat my own lamb
My own chicken and ham
I shear my own fleece and I wear it
I have lawns I have bowers
I have fruits I have flowers
The lark is my mornings alarmer
So joyfully boys now
Here's God speed the plough
Long life and success to the farmer.

As time goes by I find myself getting more and more into Green living and looking for free range poultry and eggs, organic foods environmentally friendly this and that. We have done this planet no favours and I am sure we will pay for it. The movement for free range chicken is having the desired effect. I went into Tesco's only to find they had shelves full of chickens at £1.99 each, but not one free range or organic, all were sold out. This is to me most encouraging, but why doesn't Tesco buy in enough better quality birds as there is obviously the demand for them? You can certainly tell the difference in the flavour and texture of the firmer free range bird.

As Easter draws near I think back to my youth and every Good Friday we had salt cod. Now I have found a beautiful dish using it from Provence in France, 'Brandade' served on toast or with a green salad is a very rich and comforting dish containing buttery mash with plenty of garlic, olive oil, and salty fish.

BRANDADE.

250g. Salt fish, (usually cod)
500g. floury potatoes
25g. unsalted butter
50ml. Hot milk
4-6 tablespoons olive oil
2-3 large cloves garlic chopped finely
1-2 tablespoons double cream
Freshly ground black pepper.

Soak fish in cold water for 48 hours changing the water frequently. Put fish into a pan cover with fresh water and bring to a simmer for 10-15 mins. Drain, pick over the fish removing bones and skin and break into flakes.

Boil the potatoes then mash with the butter and hot milk until soft but not sloppy.

Heat 2-3 tablespoons of olive oil in a pan over a low heat and sweat the garlic for 2-3 mins without letting it colour.

Put the flaked fish in a processor and pulse several times, trickling in the warm garlic and oil as you do so.

Now add another 2 tablespoons olive oil and the double cream and pulse again.

Transfer the pureed fish and the mash into a large bowl and combine. Place in a heatproof dish and bake for 15-20 mins at gas mark 5.

This is lovely with salad as a main course or as a starter or canapé on wholemeal toast.

Do try it for a real treat

Enjoy

Wafflings of a villager
April 2008

The first of April some do say
Is set aside for all fools day
But why the people call it so
Nor I nor they themselves do know

I shall this month graft an old variety of apple tree ie. 'Michaelmass Red' which is a very dark red / black looking apple of good flavour. This will bring my total of apples in my small garden to 9, along with 2 pears, 1 plum, 1cherry, 2 figs, 1 white and 1 brown, not to forget a hazel and 3 grapes. There is always somewhere in a garden for fruit against a panel fence or along the edge of a path as a stepover.

As I write this, 20th. February, I am ready to prick out into pots, my tomatoes and peppers, chillies and aubergines. I have just germinated some old American heritage tomatoes called 'Oregon Spring' which I saved in 1995, I thought I must have lost them, but alas although slower germinating than the others I have a fine pot of seedlings so I must save some fresh seeds this year as 13 year old seed is doing well. I have also 2 varieties of lettuce, 2 vars. Brussels sprouts, some hispi cabbage, blanch leeks, and some thyme seedlings to pot. I have sown some very old seed I have saved of some heritage broad beans and am pleased to say they too are germinating so another narrow escape with old heritage seeds. The memory lapses and the years roll on.

The Spring has sprung
The grass has riz
I wonder where the birdie is
The bird is on the wing
But that's absurd
The wing is on the bird.

I have just smoked some sprats and they went down so good. I am pleased the season is with us for Asparagus and by the time you read this I will have had a picking or two. I love it just grilled on a barred grill with butter oozing over it. With my medical problems I shouldn't have butter and to that end we bought some 'Butter Buds' it's an all American product of butter granules but all the nasties have been taken out and it has to be said the flavour isn't bad (it's not fantastic) but not bad.

There are a few good wild foods to be had in April and one of the best is the young translucent leaves of the beech. These make a fine sweet salad vegetable or can be cooked as a green veg. There is also a drink made from them called 'Beech leaf Noyau'. Pack a jar ¾ full of leaves and pour on gin. Leave for a couple of weeks then strain off the now brilliant green coloured gin and to every pint, add up to 1 lb. Sugar depending how syrupy you wish the liqueur to be dissolved in 1/2 pint boiling water. Finally add a little Brandy, mix well and bottle when cold. It is a very potent brew so be warned! The shoots of Hogweed are used like a green veg and tastes very much like asparagus. Corn salad, dandelion, hawthorn buds and lady's smock are all good food for free and at the end of the month St. Georges mushrooms will be found.

I have been pondering what to have as my recipe this month. Having read Allan Avery's 'Roughmoor Outpost' I think there may be pigeons to be had in plenty. I always squirrel away several in the freezers. So to my recipe as they are very good eating.

Pot Roast Pigeons.

4 pigeons
4 oz. Butter
12 small onions or shallots
1/2 lb. Mushrooms
4 rashers of bacon diced.
1 liqueur glass of Brandy
1 glass white wine
1 cup meat stock.
Salt and pepper to taste.

Brown the trussed pigeons in the butter and transfer to an earthenware pot into which they fit tightly

Saute briefly in the same butter, the onions and mushrooms with the bacon. Dilute the cooking juices with the brandy and wine, add the stock and bring to a boil. Season with salt and pepper and pour the contents over the pigeons.

Make sure the lid is tightly sealed and cook in the oven on mark 3 for 1 hour, an extra 20 mins. for older birds.

Do try it, and enjoy.

Wafflings of a villager
May 2008.

Up merry Spring, and up the merry
ring
For Summer is acome unto day
How happy are those little birds that merrily do
sing
On the merry morning of May.

Wild food to enjoy now is ransom's or wild
garlic, it makes a lovely soup. A herbal tea is
made with that pernicious weed 'ground ivy' and
lime leaves too make a beautiful 'green tea'.

My garden beautifies my yard
And adds fragrance to the air
But it is also my Cathedral
And my quiet place of prayer

The tomatoes are growing away in the
greenhouse with the promise of good crops of
delicious tomatoes of varied colours and taste's. I
always look forward to them probably more than
any other vegetable as they are so tasty and
versatile. Second to toms. My runner beans are
always looked forward to. We grow about 3 or 4
varieties and there are always some to give away.
I have before now when 'doing' a dinner party
even though I had made a starter and fish course
before main and desert, gone into the greenhouse
and smelt sun warmed tomatoes and picked a red,

156

pink, yellow, black, green and orange one, sliced them, picked fresh basil leaves, a few olives, crumbled some fetta cheese and dressed with olive oil and lemon juice and served a second starter still warm from the sun and how well it was received said it all, simple, tasty and light.

Ill fortune comes to those who wash clothes on May Day.

Early May is a good time to plant up your hanging baskets and tubs for a beautiful summer display. The flower show committee and Averys plant centre give vouchers for the best hanging baskets and show of flowering containers in the village, this was done to beautify our village so lets really have a go this year. These are judged to be seen from the road on the Tuesday before the flower show.

It is worth mentioning that for the celebration of the 400 years of the church bells, the flower show is having a 'Scarecrow' competition where it is hoped that villagers will make a scarecrow and exhibit it in their front garden where it can be judged. The first, second and third to make an appearance at the flower show on August 9th. We as the flower show committee are also doing a 400 year celebration of the bells by having a 'Gardeners question time' on Thursday 19th. June in the church at 7 pm. It will be a bring and share supper and we will supply drinks, admission will be free, and it is hoped that we will attract a good number of villagers and friends, further details later.

With the few nice sunny days we have had it prompted me into bricking up my new bar-b-q in readiness next to the chimnea we bought late last year. I love cooking outdoors and to this end I have started to stock up the freezer with homemade beef burgers, lamb kebabs, with cumin and coriander, marinated pork ribs and three types of sausages, pork leek garlic and herb, Sardinian with pork sun dried tomatoes, pine nuts, fennel seeds and herbs and Somerset pork with apple and cider. I have many home made beers, wines etc. so we just need some warm settled weather and we are ready for a good cook up.

Time now for my recipe of the month.

Gardeners salad, (good with the bar-b-q)

8 oz. Broad beans
8 oz. New carrots, sliced.
8 oz. New potatoes
8 oz. Cooked chicken, diced.
4 spring onions, chopped.
4 hard boiled eggs quartered.
4 tablespoons French dressing.
4 tblsp. Natural yogurt
salt and black pepper.

Cook the beans, carrots and potatoes until tender.

Dice potatoes and toss in the dressing and yogurt whilst still warm and leave to cool, then add remaining ingredients and mix well.

Serve chilled.

Enjoy.

Wafflings of a villager
June 2008.

A leak in June brings harvest soon.

As I write, not in real time but ahead of time (April) I have been given trout from you know who, well I took the sides off, boned and skinned them. I decided that one fish was too big for two so I cut off the tail ends and we had the fillets covered in a herb crust and grilled, they were beautiful with a mustard sauce and new potatoes. The tail pieces I hot smoked after curing in salt for half an hour. Suddenly I had a flash of inspiration I tried the smoked trout and it was divine. I promptly popped off to the shop and bought a tub of cottage cheese. I blitzed the trout with the cottage cheese, lemon juice and cayenne pepper and made a delicious smoked trout pate. I will definitely make that again.

24th. St. John or Midsummer day.

June is saying to me, new potatoes, new peas, new young carrots all very clean, light and tasty. It really is good to go into the garden, pick dinner, come indoors and cook and eat within half an hour. Sorry I'm getting on my soapbox about food miles again but you have to agree the difference is phenomenal.

As I sit in my conservatory (April 29th.) looking out I see my apple trees blooming, pears set, cherry in bloom, strawberries, raspberries and loganberries all promising a rich fruit harvest. I love this time of the year as all the herbs are at their best now, nice young parsley, chives, lots of young mint, beautiful soft sprigs of thyme and the sage. There are so many fresh herbs, you just want to cook. An omelette lightly cooked and a handful of chopped fresh herbs added at the very last minute is a simple but fantastic quick meal.

So to my recipe for this month. I am very fond of 'Sushi' and it is so easy as the only thing to cook is the sushi rice.

Sushi

125 gms. Sushi rice (Tesco's) sorry.
A few sheets of Nori seaweed (same place)
Wasabi paste,   "
165 mls. Water.
1 tablespoon rice wine vinegar
1 tbsp. Mirin (rice wine)
1 teaspoon sugar
1 tspn. Salt.
Put rice and the water in a pan and bring to a
boil, simmer for 10 mins. with the lid on. Turn
off the heat and leave to stand for 15-20 mins. Do
not open the lid.

Sushi dressing. In a bowl add all the other
ingredients except the seaweed and stir into the
rice. When the rice is just warm make your sushi.
Lay a sheet of nori seaweed on a bamboo rolling
mat (Tesco's). Put on a layer of rice, cut thin
strips of raw salmon or tuna also some thin strips
of cucumber and place across the width of the
rice, onto the fish add a smear of wasabi paste.

Now using the bamboo rolling mat, roll the
seaweed roll until the seaweed overlaps and seals
in the rice. Slice into 2" pieces with a very sharp
knife. Serve with a dipping sauce of soy and
mirin also pickled ginger.

Sionara

Wafflings of a Villager
July 2008.

St. Swithin's day if thou dost rain
For forty days it will remain
St. Swithin's day if thou be fair
For forty days 'twill rain nae mair

A few jobs around the garden now is to mulch
your runner beans with grass mowings, sow some
parsley for winter and spring use, spray your
tomatoes and potatoes against blight with
'Bordeaux' mixture. Time too for lifting and
dividing bearded irises. Cut out the canes that
fruited from your raspberries and tie in new
canes.

My runner beans are on schedule for picking on
the 9th. July I usually get my first picking on that
date and how I am looking forward to them. As I
write this (May 21st.) they are 3 feet high and
looking healthy. This year I have grown 7
varieties ie. Lady Di, Enorma, Sunset,
Achievement merit, Wisley Magic, Liberty and a
black seeded variety I had given me.

I have cut a good crop of asparagus during April,
May and June and with my quail laying well I
made some asparagus and quail egg tartlets
which was a 'straight from the garden dish'
which was very tasty and very local! There is so
much in the garden to eat in July that we are
spoilt for choice, including my crop of cherries.
This is a good time to take strawberry runners for

a new bed as if left year on year they do decline and often develop a virus. It's lovely to have my own tomatoes again as they are far superior to any that can be bought.

I have just made some Cornish pasties, although I do call them Somerset Tiddy Oggies. I cut thin strips of beef skirt across the grain, slice onions, swede and potatoes on a mandolin (I used to use a speed peeler), in 1/2 inch pieces and 1/8. inch thick. I cut circles or pastry about 9 inch diameter and place the mixed veg on half of the base, season with salt and black pepper, then a layer of beef strips, season salt and pepper and a dash of Lea and Perrin sauce. Another layer of potatoes, swede and onion and season again. Dot with butter and cover with the pastry and crimp. Glaze with egg wash and bake in the oven on a moderate heat for 45 mins. Stab a slit in the top.

I would like to take this opportunity to thank everyone involved with the 'Bishop's Hull Memoirs' film premier at the Manor, and for the staff who did us proud with the food and drinks and hospitality. It was a super night and was lovely to have a natter to 'old friends', some I went to Bishop's Hull school with over 60 years ago.

So to my recipe of the month and its Editor Bob's Favourite, I make this often, changing the seafood ie. Squid, octopus, scallops etc.

SPANISH PAELLA.

4 chicken legs cut in two
2 oz. Butter.
1 tablespoon olive oil.
6 oz. Onion.
2 cloves garlic (crushed).
4 oz. Chorizo. Sliced thickly.
8 oz. Paella rice.
1/2 teaspoon saffron.
1 pint chicken stock.
1 pepper (any colour).
1 level teaspoon salt and one of pepper.
6 oz. Cooked peas, fresh or frozen.
4 oz. Peeled prawns.
4 oz. Lobster or white crabmeat.
To garnish, 12 fresh mussels and 8 unpeeled
prawns.

Put oil and butter in a pan and fry chicken joints
until brown and crispy then remove, add onion
and garlic and fry until golden. Slice chorizo and
add to pan with the rice and saffron. Mix in well
cover with stock, bring to a boil stirring.

Add chopped pepper and simmer for 10 mins.

Add salt and stand chicken joints on top of the
rice, cover with a lid and cook in the oven for 40
mins at 180c. gas mark 4.

Uncover and sprinkle with peas and prawns then add crabmeat. Check that the chicken is done.

10 mins. before serving, put the cleaned mussels in a pan with 2 tablespoons of wine or water, cover and shake the pan over a brisk heat until shells open. Add to the top of the Paella together with the unpeeled prawns. Sprinkle with chopped parsley and invite me around.

Enjoy.

Wafflings of a Villager
August 2008

Harvest home.
Dry August and warm does harvest no harm.

In the garden there is still plenty to do, sow green top turnips for winter greens, sow winter spinach also carrot and beets for early Autumn use, feed leeks with a weak liquid manure and prune your rambling roses. There is still time to plant out kales and winter cabbage. While crops are bountiful it is well worth making chutneys, pickles etc. to be put by for leaner times, it's when the cooking apples are plentiful I make brown sauce for the year also with tomatoes I make ketchup and tomato / chilli jam.

Tomatoes, particularly the cherry type are worth bottling. His year I have grown a small Italian cucumber called 'cucino'. It's about 4 inches long and they produce like crazy so I have pickled some of these. Some of the new variety veg is well worth trying. We tend to grow 'the old favourites' but for instance this year I grew a courgette that needs no pollinating, so every fruit sets and I was picking courgettes in May together with the mini cucumber.

Wild mushrooms should be about now and the ceps and chicken of the woods is well worth finding so a stroll through a broad leaf wood should be rewarding. One day our great grandchildren could be gathering fungi from our own Bishop's Hull wood at Netherclay, as well as chestnuts and hazels.

I am trying an old North American Indian way of growing their three staples, ie. Beans, sweet corn and squashes, in a method that was known as the three sisters. Firstly, sweet corn was planted, then climbing beans were grown up the corn and finally it was under planted with squashes. I have obtained some of the old heritage beans called' Cherokee trail of tears' it's a bit of living history and I will report on how it goes. If I go to Wallaces farm shop and buy some bison, I could have a complete Red Indian meal.

Our village flower show is on the 9th. August and entries must be in by Monday 4th. August so you haven't long now, do have a go. We are looking forward to seeing how the Scarecrow competition goes and hopefully it could be ongoing with a different theme every year, as you know this year is a scarecrow with a bell. One of our classes in the show schedule is a photograph of a 2008 village event a theme for a floral art exhibit is church bells so we are still celebrating 2008.

We are in high summer and outdoor eating and picnics are a treat so for my recipe of the month I will share with you a tasty country meat loaf which can be eaten hot or cold with salad.

COUNTRY MEAT LOAF.

1 oz. Butter
1 onion finely chopped
2 cloves garlic crushed
2 celery sticks finely chopped
1lb. Lean minced beef
1lb. Minced pork
2 eggs
2oz. Fresh white breadcrumbs
3tablespoons chopped fresh parsley
2tbls. Fresh snipped basil
1teaspoon fresh thyme leaves
1/2 teaspoon salt
1/2 teaspoon ground black pepper
2tbsps. Worcester sauce
4 tbsps. chilli sauce or ketchup
6 rind less streaky bacon rashers.
Fresh basil sprigs to garnish.

Pre heat oven to 180c. gas mark 4.

Melt butter in the pan and fry onion, garlic and celery on a low heat to sweat until softened. Remove from heat. In a large mixing bowl combine the onion, garlic and celery with all the other ingredients except the bacon and mix well together.

Use your hands to shape the mixture into an oval loaf. Put into a roasting tin and lay the slices of bacon across the meat loaf and bake for 1.1/2. hours, basting occasionally.

Remove from the oven and drain off the fat.
Place the meat loaf on a platter and leave to stand
for 10 minutes before serving if hot or leave to get
cold and slice, then garnish with basil.

Serve cold with salad or hot with new potatoes
and peas, beans etc.

Enjoy

Wafflings of a villager
September 2008.

September blow soft
Till the fruits are in the loft.

It will soon be time to pick in some of your
apples to store in a cool shed. I usually wrap
mine in newspaper first and just keep an eye on
them from time to time. My favourite is an old
French variety called 'Orleans Reinette' which is
good at Christmas with Stilton and a glass of
Port. Last month I was given some frogs legs so I
sautéed them in butter dipped in flour with diced
mushrooms, croutons, fresh parsley, chives,
garlic and tarragon and finished with lemon juice,
they were beautiful.
 The garden has been producing wonderful crops
of potatoes, cabbages, shallots, sweetcorn,
courgettes, cucumbers, tomatoes, aubergines,
asparagus, dwarf beans, broad beans, runner
beans, peas, lettuce, peppers, chillies, etc. not to
mention raspberries, loganberries, strawberries
and cherries. Still to harvest sprouts, purple
sprouting, Kales, leeks and celery, winter
spinach, cima di rapa, (an Italian green) and bulb
fennel. There is still time to sow some parsley
and chervil for winter use also lettuce and winter
hardy 'spring onions' and plant too some spring
cabbages. The older gardeners used to have a
trick or two up their sleeves for making the best
of everything, and one tip I was given as a boy

171

was to cut off the tops of turnips now then trim off the leaves and the slices of turnip that we were left (the top slice with the leaf bases intact) were planted in boxes of compost and put in a warm shed and this would force the new shoots, which because of lack of light were cream coloured and very tender and unusual as a veg. All sorts of root veg were stored in boxes of sand for winter use, like carrots, beets, swede and turnips. Parsnips are left in the ground to get frosted as when this happens the sugars set in the flesh and make them lovely and sweet.

Now the weather is cooling down and flies are diminishing it will be time for me to make my salami's and chorizo for my paella. It's made from minced pork and diced back fat with red wine, hot and sweet paprika, salt, Prague powder (a preservative), pepper and this is mixed and stuffed into beef runners (intestines), tied and hung outdoors to air dry for about 2-3 months. They keep once made for several months.

Another thing I do at this time is to make pickles and chutneys for Christmas and the New Year as there are lots of spare vegetables and fruits at this time. I will certainly be making some sweet piccalilli with cauliflower, cucumber, courgette, small shallots, and runner beans as this always goes well with cold meats and terrines.

Blackberry and apple tarts go down well and it's well worth the effort of going into the hedgerows and gathering some of natures harvest. And talking of natures harvest, it will be soon time to go to the woods and collect chestnuts for the turkey stuffings. When you have collected them, leave them outdoors preferably on the garden where they will keep well.

Thus harvest ends it's busy reign
And leaves the fields their peace again.

Well to my recipe of the month and I thought I had done Spanish and Japanese So here's my Indian Chicken Korma with Naan breads. My young grandsons make this when they come for a stopover, one makes the curry and the other, the Naan breads, they swap over next time around.

Chicken Korma.

1 Tablespoon oil
4 chicken breasts cut into chunks
2 onions chopped
2 cloves garlic chopped
some small button mushrooms
about an ounce of ground almonds
a small pot of natural yoghurt
1.1/2. dessertspoons of medium curry powder.
1 teaspoon turmeric
salt and pepper
a little water
2 tablespoons of cream to finish.

Sweat the onions and garlic in the oil, when soft
add chopped chicken and stir until opaque. Add
turmeric and curry powder and stir for a moment
to cook the spices. Add the yoghurt and enough
water to come level to the chicken. Add salt and
pepper to taste. Simmer on a low heat for about
40 mins.

Meanwhile, fry the mushrooms and add to the
curry together with the ground almonds, stir in
well and add the cream, stir and serve with
basmati rice and Naan breads.

Naan Breads

1 lb. Strong white flour
10 fld. Oz. Lukewarm water
1 sachet easyblend yeast
1 teaspoon salt
Melted butter
A little yoghurt
You can add chopped coriander, garlic and black onion seeds for a top of the range Naan.

Mix all the ingredients except butter together and knead until the dough becomes elastic. Leave to rise until double the size. Knock back and divide the dough into tennis ball size, then roll out into elongated ovals. Brush with melted butter and place on baking sheets.

When they have risen, place into a pre-heated oven at 200 degrees, gas mark 6 for around 12 mins. If not lightly brown, give them a few more minuets. When out of the oven brush them again with melted butter.

Enjoy

Wafflings of a villager
October 2008

I love this time of year as some of my favourite
foods come into season. Pheasants, wood pigeon,
woodcock, rabbits, Brussels sprouts, salsify, and
scorzonera, apples, chestnuts and damsons,
pumpkins etc. There are still wild mushrooms to
gather and one of my favourite starters that I still
get asked for is my 'cornucopia de fungi De bois'
which is mixed wild mushrooms in a creamy
sauce and stuffed into puff pastry horns and
spilling onto the plate

When chestnut leaves do fall
Cotton ain't no good at all.

I love to make a pasta dish with the squashes that
are now available to us. I make a butternut squash
ravioli with a sage butter sauce and it is really
very good and simple to make.
For the pasta I use 1 large egg to 100gms pasta
flour, mix well and knead until quite firm, now
leave to rest. Meanwhile I roast the squash until
tender, mash with butter and add Parmesan
cheese and season with salt, pepper and nutmeg.
Next, get your pasta dough and roll it very
thinly. (I use a pasta roller.) With a scone cutter I
cut 2 inch circles, which then have a spoonful of
the filling, then brush around the edges with
water and the second circle placed over the top
and pressed down around the edges to seal. Next,

melt the butter and add some young sage leaves
and fry for a few minutes. Boil the ravioli for
around 4 minutes and then drain and add sage
butter sauce, and a grating of Parmasan. It is a
very simple but tasty dish.

Nature now spread, around in dreamy hue
A pall to cover all that summer knew.

There is plenty to do in the garden still and now
is a good time to dig manure into the ground to
ensure a fertile soil for next year's crops, as I
believe there is no better 'fertilizer' and have
ordered 20 sacks. I do use compost bins to add
extra humus to the soil, as every bit you put into
the garden will pay you back with good crops.
Time to lift and divide perennials like
michaelmas daisies, scabious, phlox, etc, and cut
out side thongs of Oriental poppies, lupin and
anchusa.
Plant some garlic, spring cabbage and sow some
over wintering lettuce seeds. I grow one called
'valdor' with great success as they produce large
butter head salads of good flavour. Also winter
hardy \spring onions'. It is not too late to plant
wallflowers, violas and spring bulbs for a
colourful spring show. It's the time to prune your
black, red and white currants, also pears and
gooseberries to keep them producing well.

The three ages of countrymen.

At heart we are all countrymen, it's just that
some have lost their roots
And need reminding of days when, grandfathers
walked in greener boots.

In childhood leads life's dance as green ways
beg us to explore,
And every season brings romance but summer
lasts for evermore.

In middle age we drift away in search of gold
and more and more
And even on our better days see country fields as
factory floor.

But in old age romance returns to haunt the
heart of yesteryear
And then the countryman soon yearns for fields
he once held dear.

SWEET AND SOUR PORK, CHICKEN CHOP SUEY AND YOUNG CHOW FRIED RICE

sweet and sour pork

8oz pork fillet

a small amount of batter and for the sauce:

2 tbsp wine vinegar
3 tbsp sugar
3 tbsp orange juice
1 tbsp tomato puree
1 1/2 tbsp soy sauce
1 1/2 tbsp dry sherry or rice wine
1 tbsp cornflour
5 tbsps water or pineapple juice

Combine all sauce ingredients, bring to a boil,
stirring all the time, and reserve.
Cut the pork into 1 inch cubes, dip into batter
and deep fry until golden.

Drain and reserve.

chicken chop suey

2 chicken breasts thinly sliced and marinated in
a little cornflour and soy sauce for an hour.
Half an onion, sliced
3 – 4 mushrooms, sliced.

1 tin mixed Chinese vegetables (bean sprouts, bamboo shoots, etc.)
1 clove garlic chopped, plus a thumb of ginger, shredded.
3 tbsp hoi sin sauce.
A few splashes of spy sauce and pepper.

Heat wok to hot, add a little groundnut oil and stir fry the garlic and ginger. Add chicken and cook until opaque.

Now add the onion and mushrooms and stir fry. Add the drained can of vegetables and fry for a few minutes, add hoi sin and soy sauce, bring to a boil and keep warm.

young chow friend rice

Basmati rice cooked 1 hour before it is required and spread out on a tray to dry.
1 doz. cooked prawns
2 spring onions, chopped.
2 tbsp frozen peas
1 rasher of bacon, chopped
a little chopped meat, ie: chicken, ham, etc.
1 beaten egg
soy sauce
a dash of sesame oil if possible to finish.

Add a little oil to the wok and add prawns, onions, peas, bacon, meats and stir fry for 1 minute.

Now add beaten egg and stir until cooked.

Add rice and stir fry until hot, add a few splashes of soy to colour slightly.

Finally, add a splash of sesame oil to season.

Enjoy.

Wafflings of a Villager
November 2008.

Now boys with squibs and crackers play
And bonfires blaze turns night into day.

There is so much in season now and as the
colder weather draws near, warming comfort
food is the order of the day. We now have at our
disposal many winter vegetables and glorious
game.
So many home cooked substantial meals can be
made, and why not make more than needed then
some can go into the freezer for a busy day in the
future.

A lot of the cheaper cuts of meat are very tasty
but need a longer cooking time so whilst you are
cooking them, it makes sense to cook at least
twice as much to save fuel. The sorts of cuts I use
are oxtail, beef skirt, brisket, ox cheek (if you can
get it,) is so flavourful, I know Donald Russell
sells it (try the website.) Scrag end of lamb, ideal
for Lancashire hot pot, ox hearts stuffed and
braised is beautiful, slow roasted belly pork and
pigs cheeks (bath chaps), skinned and cured for
48 hours in salt and salt petre, cooked for three
hours, rolled in breadcrumbs and allowed to cool.
I made some in September as my Piccalilli was
just about ready and it was good to eat cold with
a salad.

11ᵗʰ. November St. Martin

It is the day of Martilmasse,
Cuppes of ale should freelie passé
What through Wynter has begunne
To push downe the summer sunne
To our fire we can betake
And enjoy the crackling brake
Never headinge Wynters face
On the day of Martilmasse

I must admit that I am now getting quite exited about Christmas as I do every year. Time to order the poultry from Tim and start to think about the family coming to stay, with the expectation of good food and drink. I would like a goose this year but fear it would not be big enough and to have a goose for one day and turkey for the other would seem overindulgence. I usually make my mini chipolata sausages rolled in my home dry cured bacon and freeze them and also make two stuffing's for the turkey ie. chestnut and sage and onion, one for the body cavity and the other for the neck end. If we have a goose I like an apple, prune and Armagnac stuffing in the body and sage and onion in the neck end. Last year I smoked a pheasant and made some smoked pheasant pate and it was a resounding success, but I make that just a few days before.

183

On the first of November if the weather hold
clear
An end of what sowing you do for this year.

In the garden now it is advisable to dig over any vacant ground, adding manure or compost if possible. You can now sow longpod broad beans on a sheltered site and plant shallots and garlic. I like to lift some mint roots and box up under cold glass for winter use, although I have squirreled some away in the freezers as ice cubes and as a second back up I do make an apple and mint jelly too.

Parsley can be lifted and potted up and put in a cold greenhouse to provide fresh parsley through the winter. It's a good time too for staking tall varieties of Brussels sprouts to save them from rocking around. You can now prune grape vines under glass. When I was a lad it was quite usual to lift runner bean roots now and plant them in boxes under glass so they had an early crop the next year, it's a way of growing not used much today.

There is still time for wild mushrooms like hedgehog, blewits, parasols etc. and what flavour they deliver, out of this world compared to button mushrooms. I have too picked sloes, bullaces and chestnuts in November. Rabbits, pigeons, pheasants etc. are all wild foods and through the Autumn and Winter they are a very tasty and inexpensive meat which goes well with the seasonal vegetables. I mentioned that I would tell how my North American Native Indian growing system trial progressed. This was the system called 'Three sisters' which was growing their three staples. Sweetcorn was planted and to this climbing beans ('Cherokee trail of tears') grew up the corn. Under this block, three squashes were planted. It all seemed very feasible and all got off to a good start. Unfortunately on the seed packet they did not give a height for the sweetcorn, (I was thinking the usual six feet) it however only managed 3 feet so the beans climbed to the top quite happily then sprawled all over. I firstly picked the corn, which was delicious, picked and cooked within 10 minutes. Later the beans came into bear and very nice they were too. Finally the squashes developed and we have 'carnival' and 'Turks turban' the third was 'Butternut' and I didn't see the going of that one. So all in all it was a success and to have three crops on one area of garden is using the ground to it's maximum.

In our food trip abroad I forgot Italy so here is my very own recipe for Spaghetti Bolognese.

My Spaghetti Bolognese.

8 oz. Minced beef
2 sticks celery chopped
1 large onion chopped
2 cloves garlic chopped
8 oz. Minced pork
tablespoon olive oil
4 oz. Chicken livers chopped.
3 good sized tomatoes or tin chopped.
2 rashers streaky bacon chopped.
A little milk
1 glass red wine
salt and pepper
fresh basil leaves or dried marjoram.
Teaspoon sugar
2 tablespoons tomato puree.
Dash of Worcester sauce.

Fry the onions, garlic and celery in the oil until
transparent. Add meats and fry those until
browned. Add a spot of milk and bring to a boil
and simmer for a few mins.

Now add the tomatoes, wine, sauce, tomato
puree, sugar, basil salt and pepper. Bring to a
simmer and cook very low for at least one hour,
the longer the better.

Drop the pasta into boiling salted water and cook
until done. Put spaghetti onto the plates top with

the ragu sauce and sprinkle with grated parmesan cheese.

Enjoy, Fantastico.

Wafflings of a Villager December 2008.

At Christmas play and make good cheer
For Christmas comes but once a year.

Well here we are once more, the end of the year
and how the years slip away. I well remember at
the age of four at St. Johns school having a
Christmas party with marionettes, tableau's and
dressing up as shepherds. We had taken 2.oz. lard
and 1 oz. Sugar so we could have a large cake
made, (it was at the end of the war). Also our
Christmas parties at Bishop's Hull old school
where just once a year we could have the gas
lights on, it was magical. I do love Christmas, as
any of my family will tell. The carols played
from early November, the making sure that my
family is well catered for. When I was a lad,
Christmas was so much more simple, for instance
in my stocking there would be from my
Grandmother six halfpennies that had been shone
up with Brasso, then the rest of my stocking
contained a few almonds, a few lead soldiers, a
book and crayons and an orange. No computer
games etc. What a simple and pleasurable life we
led.

In the garden we have been enjoying, kales,
Brussels sprouts, cabbages, celery and some store
vegetables. In my shed there is my eating apples
and cooking apples, my Orleans Reinettes will be
out for Christmas with some Colston Basset
Stilton and a glass of Port. Believe it or not

Boxing Day is the day to sow your large onion seed under glass. My garlic is around a foot high and looking good. There are plenty of herbs to pick including lots of parsley which I could not be without. I have it growing in the herb bed, in a large pot in the greenhouse, a hanging basket under cover and a planter on the wall so I should not run out. Thyme is my next most used herb and so I have five plants, which keep me with plenty, and just taken some more cuttings. Bay is no problem as one tree gives more than could ever be used. These three herbs are the classical bouquet garni and is a basic for all-serious cooking. The lettuces I sowed in September are hearting up and we will shortly be cutting those in the greenhouse border where they will be replaced by tomatoes.

The fare for Christmas has changed too over the years, it's all turkey now but I was about sixteen years before I tasted turkey. We used to have geese for Christmas dinner and my father would bring home two goslings from the market and it was my job to look after them and make sure they were in their hut by night. Then a few days before the 25th. They would be killed, plucked and drawn for our dinner. We had two geese, as there were six of us plus occasionally my Grandmother. On Boxing Day it was a tradition in our house to roast a few rabbits in the goose grease and they tasted fantastic. Needless to say all the vegetables came from the garden.

It was when at sixteen another apprentice printing mate who lived in Beer Crowcombe had a smallholding and his father sold turkeys at Christmas so I bought one of his and took home to my Mother for a change. I can remember it weighed 23lbs. And cost a whopping 3 guineas (I was then earning £2/10 s. a week). Mother had to hang it in the oven from a wire coat hanger to cook it, but I remembered it tasted fantastic and we did the same meat for several years then I yearned for a goose again.

We would always roast the chestnuts we collected in October as we had a range with an oven to one side and it roasted chestnuts beautifully also jacket potatoes. We always had, as I do still, a ham, jellied ox tongue and home made pates and terrines. We also had large stone jars with paraffin wax covered tops full of pickled shallots, pickled red cabbage and mixed mustard pickles.

Back in October we made our Christmas puddings, mini chipolatas wrapped in bacon and the two stuffing's are put away in the freezer. I also made some of 'Delias' spiced pickled pears which are nice with cold meats such as ham etc. or with 'Roquefort' and salad as a starter.

Before I offer my recipe of the month I would like to apologise for the omission of a vital ingredient from last months Spaghetti Bolognese, this was some stock. I did phone Bob, but alas it had, the day before, gone to the printers.

And so to my recipe.

A nice light fish gougere for the Christmas season.

2 tbsp. Plain flour
1/2 tbspn. Salt
4.1/2. oz. Butter
7 fld. Oz. Water
3 beaten eggs
5 oz. Gruyere cheese grated.
9 oz. Smoked haddock
1 bay leaf.
8 fld. Oz. Milk.
1 small red onion chopped.
5 oz. Button mushrooms, sliced.
1 teaspoon mild curry powder
fresh lemon juice.
2 tbsp. Fresh parsley chopped.
Salt and ground black pepper.

Lightly grease a shallow ovenproof dish.
On to a plate sieve 3.3/4. oz flour and add salt.
Put 3 oz. Of butter into a pan add the water and heat gently.
Bring to a boil, tip in the flour mix and beat well.
When the mixture leaves the side of the pan, take off the heat and cool for five minuets.
Slowly work in the beaten egg, beating well.
Now stir in two thirds of the grated cheese.
Spoon the choux pastry around the edge of the dish making sure it comes up the sides well.
Pre heat oven to mark 4, 180c.

Put haddock, bay leaf and milk in pan and cover and bake for 15 mins.

Lift out the fish but reserve milk. Melt remaining butter in a frying pan, add mushrooms and sauté for about 5 mins.

Mix in remaining flour and curry powder (if using).

Gradually stir in the milk and stir until smooth. Add lemon juice, parsley, salt and pepper to taste. Increase oven heat to gas mark 6. 200c.

Flake fish and add to centre of the pastry along with the mushrooms, mix spreading evenly. Sprinkle with rest of the cheese and bake for 35-40 mins. Serve.

Enjoy.

I would like to take this opportunity to wish you all a very happy, healthy and peaceful Christmas and a very happy New Year.

Artisan cooking and processing
January.

A very happy New Year to both of my readers.
What can possibly be in season in January I hear
you ask?
 Well we are not so well provided for after the
luxuries of the summer glut, but we have the
foods need for winter like Jerusalem artichokes,
Brussels sprouts, cabbages in variety, celery,
chicory, endive, kales, leeks, lettuce, onions,
parsnips, potatoes and Swedes. Fruit in season
are pears Concorde, Doyenne du Comice,
Conference, Winter Nellis, chestnuts and forced
rhubarb. Fish, cod, cockles, crab, Whiting,
oysters, Game available, Hare, rabbit, partridge,
Pheasant, snipe and woodcock.
 As we see, there is not as much choice but with a
bit of imagination many fantastic meals can be
cooked from what is available now. In the colder
weeks ahead we fall back on stews and
casseroles. A good oxtail casserole or a beef,
lamb or even a venison stew is hearty and
warming on a cold day. It's a good time of year
for things like steak and kidney pudding, not
really a summers dish but comfort food now.
 We have only one month left to enjoy pheasant
until the close of the season and plain roasted
with stuffing and a rasher or two of bacon on top
is a real treat, so if you haven't yet tried one, do
give one a go. I assure you that you will not be
disappointed and Tim our butcher usually has

them. I assure you I get nothing from our shops for mentioning them but when you have good shops on your doorstep and a friendly face to serve you, its got to be the best way of shopping. I can pop into the butchers and say, "that was a beautiful piece of fore rib we had on Sunday" or into Karl's and take advantage of 3 bottles of Shiraz for a tenner. You cannot go into the supermarket and remark on a joint, as it would mean nothing to the person on the counter, as they wouldn't know where the meat comes from. A classic was when a friend asked the girl on the deli counter:

" Where do these olives come from"?

"Out the back" was the reply.

January for me is the start of the sowing year and onions, some tomatoes, peppers, chillies and aubergines are sown now. My garlic was planted in November and that is now 4 inches high. Shallots will go in soon and so the New Year begins. We are still using seasonal greens etc. from the garden like my favourite kale 'Pentland brig' its much better in my mind than the tough curly kales also Brussels sprouts still plenty to pick, I also grow extra herbs for winter use as they don't replenish themselves as quickly in the cooler months. Parsley, chervil and a pot or two of mint is always there.

Well it's time for my first recipe of the year and for this you will need a rabbit, (see Tim the butcher).

Rabbit pudding with mushrooms.

1 rabbit cut into joints, or if preferred meat taken
from the bone.
A few slices of fat bacon.
8 sage leaves chopped fine.
1 small onion chopped
1/2 lb. Mushrooms.
Salt and pepper.
Suet crust, 1/2 lb. Suet to 1/2 lb. Flour.

Line a good sized pudding basin with the suet
crust.
Now put in a layer of rabbit, chopped sage and
onion and season, then a layer of mushrooms and
bacon until the basin is filled. Sprinkle plenty of
flour between each layer as that will give a good
thick gravy.
Nearly fill the basin with water or stock then
cover with the suet crust. Cover basin with foil
and steam for at least three hours, it will not spoil
if you leave it 4 or even 5 hours.
Serve with roast potatoes and vegetables of your
choice.

This is a very tasty and nourishing dish so enjoy.
Roy Baker.

WAFFLINGS
OF
A
VILLAGER

2009

Wafflings of a Villager
January 2009

Can I wish you all a very happy, healthy and
peaceful New Year.

Well we head off into another year with hope
and expectations. My expectations are in fact
very few as I just hope that life will just carry on
as usual and that my garden keeps producing
fantastic crops. With good culture and good
fertile soil we have set the scene.
 This is the start of my gardening year as onion
seeds, some early tomatoes, early summer
cabbage like 'Hispi' are sown now along with
some cauliflower and lettuce. I only have room
for a couple rows of early potatoes but even these
are bought now and laid out to chit. My favourite
early is 'Accent' as the slugs seem to leave it
alone and its wireworm and scab resistant and has
a good taste.
 I love the thought of sowing vegetable seeds and
watching them germinate and grow on into good
tasty food, and because you have chosen them as
they are your to your taste, you know exactly
what to expect. Last year I grew a new tomato to
me and it was a beautiful yellow / orange fruit of
7 oz. Called 'Caro Rich' which tasted really very
good, so that's another one to grow this year. I
have at least 40 varieties of tomato, which I keep
and usually grow only 15 varieties every year,
but it's so hard to chose which to grow and which

to leave out. I did see an article in the news that a new purple tomato has been genetically modified to give cancer beating properties, but even with the supposed technology I am personally against it. I do grow purple tomatoes including brown, white, pink, yellow, orange and green etc. But these are natural tomatoes from around the world. Whilst on the gardening tract, I would say that it's a good time now to lift and divide rhubarb also to force it by omitting light.

5th. January, Twelfth night.

Health to thee good apple tree
Whence thou may'st bud and whence thou
may'st blow
Hats full, caps full
Three bushel bags full
And my pockets full too.

Wassail the trees, that they may bear
Many a plum ,and many a pear
For more or less fruits they will bring
As you do give them Wassailing.

We are now spoilt for choice with the game that is in season and very good it is too. I have squirreled away in the freezers a good store of pheasants, partridges, pigeons, rabbits etc, so I can enjoy them 'out of season' as well. Mallard duck is a treat too and I often finish off the roasting time with a spoonful of homemade marmalade. In the past when I have had a lot of rabbits I have boned them and made bunny burgers and bunny bangers, but I like them best after all these years stuffed, and plain roasted with bacon and onions over them or a good rabbit stew with turnips, carrots, onions, and cider.

As the days lengthen
So does the cold strengthen.

It is certainly the time of year for all the comfort meals like long cooked beef stews anything up to four hours, steak and kidney puddings, (I usually have a good dollop of tomato ketchup in the stock), a slow cooked oxtail stew or casserole is a tasty treat. I made a Lancashire hot pot with some neck of lamb chops, potato slices, sliced onions and a few lamb kidneys and it was beautiful and just what was needed on that cold day.
I love experimenting with different foods and at the moment I am looking at a Spanish winter stew of 'Alubias' beans called 'Fabada' It's the beans, chorizo, black pudding, bacon, a ham hock, a pigs trotter, onions, garlic, paprika, saffron, olive oil and seasonings and they are all cooked until meltingly tender. I have a Spanish neighbour who is going to cook it for me first. She has brought me back various ingredients from Spain including some 'Iberico' sausage and chorizo.
As a boy I was taught a number of gardening tips from my mates father, Charlie Smith and when I

199

asked about budding roses he got me to see his Father in law, Mr. Rugg who lived in what is now the lower rooms of the Constitutional club. He was a very nice 'old man' and had an allotment then down on the Silk Mills road next to Bonds Dairy. Well he took me around the lanes in October to dig out some wild rose briers. We then planted them on his allotment. In late June he told me to meet him on his plot and he showed me how he took the bud from a named rose and budded it onto one of the wild briers that we had collected. He used to take the wood from bud away with a sharpened goose quill. It was good the next year to see our new rose flowering.

Mr. Rugg grew his own tobacco and cured it as he used to smoke quite big cigarettes, he lived into his 90s. It is now time for my recipe of the month so here is the first for 2009. It's an old favourite but you do need very good sausages so I make my own, why don't you give it a try?

Toad in the hole with onion gravy, fried apple rings and sage.

Beef stock
2 onions sliced thinly
5 oz. Plain flour
1/2 teaspoon salt
2 eggs lightly beaten
6 fld. Oz. Milk
2 fld. Oz. Water.
2 tablespoons oil
1 lb. Good pork sausages.
Fresh sage leaves
Apple rings fried in butter.

Put flour and salt in a bowl, add the eggs stir then add milk and water and whisk well, cover and rest for 30 mins. meanwhile pre heat the oven 220 mark 7.

Pour the oil into a roasting tin and heat tin for five minuets. Now arrange sausages in tin and cook in the oven for 10 mins.

Whisk the batter again, then quickly pour over the sausages, and return to the oven. Cook for 35 mins until golden and risen.

For the onion gravy slice the onions and fry gently in oil and butter until soft brown and sweet. Add a little flour to thicken then add a

little beef stock and a teaspoon of mustard. Bring
to a boil to thicken the gravy.

Serve the toad in the hole garnished with apple
rings, sage leaves and onion gravy.
Enjoy

Wafflings of a Villager
February 2009

2nd. Candlemas

If Candlemas be fair and clear
We'll have two winters in one year.

February the first is the end of the pheasant
season but rabbits are still available and I do
enjoy a rabbit stuffed with sage and onion,
covered in onions and bacon and roasted slowly.
I can usually find one in my freezers.
  I have dug in a mountain of manure so the
ground should be in good heart for the oncoming
planting of vegetables. My tomato seedlings are
ready to pot on as are my peppers, chillies and
aubergines. They are so useful when the
courgettes and cucumbers come to fruition.
  I have also sown some early Brussels sprouts,
summer cabbages and my broad beans. I prefer to
sow broad beans in February then I can grow the
green seeded and tasty ones like Dobies rentpayer
and Masterpiece green long pod which are in my
opinion much better than the Autumn sown
Aquadulce which is a white seeded tasteless one
by comparison.
  I am too taking cuttings of my early bloom
chrysanthemums now. It's a good time to get
those roses, shrubs and fruit trees planted up. My
old Victorian Parma Violet ''the Czar' is
flowering now and when I was a boy my mother

used to make me a birthday cake and she usually
decorated it with candied violets as it was her
favourite flower and they flowered for my
Birthday.

But hark I hear the pancake bell
And fritters make a gallant smell
The cooks are baking, frying, boyling
Stewing, mincing, cutting, broiling
Carving, gormandising, roasting
Carbonading, cracking, slashing, toasting.

When I was a lad we would go to the Brickyard
on the Wellington Road as there were mates who
lived in the row of brickyard cottages, alas long
gone now and we knew the men that worked
there as they were all local chaps, so we would
go down the pit where they dug out the clay. It
was put into small trucks. These were attached to
chains and they were pulled up a steep ramp to
the brick making sheds at the top. Well it was
great fun to get in an empty one and have a ride
up to the top.
 Occasionally when we wore out our welcome we
would go to the old area that had been cleared or
clay and it filled with water. This was surrounded
by tipped rubbish and it was easy to find a few tin
oil barrels and we would lash them together with
ropes and bicycle inner tubes and build a raft.
The fly in the ointment, there was a pair of swans
who, when breeding took umbrage at us being
there and drove us away. When cold or wet we

used to jump on a trolley and drive around the very warm kilns and we would imagine being bricked up in there.

As a teenager I would go square dancing in the old hall behind " Snail creep" with girls and boys from the village and the caller was Miss Reed who also did the school bank. Rev. Mullins was always there in attendance to keep an eye on things. It was dancing to records and we did have good times doing the 'dip and dive', 'waltz country dance', 'gay gordens', 'Valetta' etc. and when we were a little older we went ballroom dancing to the T.A. hall and into town to the Empire and Dellers.

Forced rhubarb is now available and what a treat to have these lovely pink, tender stems. Hare, mallard, partridge and pheasant are now about to go into frozen mode as February is the end of the season, but rabbits are still available. Some early purple sprouting is around now and of course we still have Brussels sprouts, Savoy cabbage and kales in the garden. To say onions are in season is not true but at this time they add warmth with a depth of flavour and body which is brought to many dishes and even on their own, roasted with thyme butter are fantastic and what a beautiful soup they make with cheesy croutons.

This brings me nicely on to my recipe for the month which is:

Rabbit Pudding with mushrooms

1 Rabbit cut into joints
a few slices of fat bacon.
6 large sage leaves chopped finely.
An onion, chopped
Pepper and salt to taste.
1/2 lb. Suet.
1/2 Lb. Flour
A good few mushrooms sliced.

Line a pudding basin with a suet crust and put in
a layer of rabbit, chopped sage and onion, then a
layer of sliced mushrooms and bacon and a
sprinkling of flour to thicken the gravy. Continue
to layer up the basin.
Nearly fill the basin with stock or water, cover
with the suet crust and steam for about 3 hours or
more for a beautiful tasty dish.

Serve it with lightly steamed kale and new
potatoes.

Enjoy

Wafflings of a Villager,
March 2009.

1st. St. David

Upon St. Davids day
Put oats and barley in the clay.

Well here we are 'March', so spring is just
around the corner and it will be most welcome, so
let us hope for a good Spring and Summer where
we can cook and eat outdoors. Last year we only
found one occasion to cook on the chimnea and
Barbie.
Not a great deal in season at the moment but
purple sprouting broccoli is around and wild
garlic or ransom's is out there for the gathering
and both nettles and wild garlic is very tasty. I
make a soup with the garlic and a blue cheese and
nettle ravioli or gnocchi. Kales and sprouts are
going out of season as is leeks, parsnips and to
my dismay, mussels which I shall miss.

As a sweet pledge of spring the little lambs,
Bleat in the varied weather round their dams.

With the credit crunch beginning to bite, it
would be a perfect time to grow a few vegetables
to help out the cost of living. Now is a good time
of the year to make a start, for instance a patio
could be dotted with grow bags and containers of
all shapes and sizes. An old compost bag will

grow a few good feeds of 'new potatoes', old buckets (with a hole in) will grow a good amount of tomatoes another would house a courgette plant. Window boxes for salad crops, lettuce, spring onions, radish etc. Some runner beans would grow in a flower tub, and so on.

If you can devote a vegetable plot, then there is so much to grow and save yourself a lot of money and have first class fresh veg that will be the envy of all your friends. Try varieties like mixed salad bowl cut and come again lettuces, Amsterdam forcing carrot, red and white flowered runner beans, 'painted lady', boltardy beetroots, white Lisbon salad onions, and the tomatoes of your choice but generally 'gardeners delight' and Alicante are easily available as plants.

March comes in like an adders head
And goes out with a peacocks tail.

As I sit in my conservatory writing this, I see a pair of blackcaps, a woodland bird really and every year I stand up the tops including the berries of my asparagus tops which they seem to find and devour with relish. Whilst on the subject of asparagus, it will be in season very soon and I get a very good harvest every year from the end of March until the back end of June and I love it.

Butcher, butcher give us a sheep's head
We can't afford best meat

But butcher, butcher don't take the eyes out
It has to see us right through the week.

I have just been given some pheasants (I am writing this at the end of January so still in season) and one of them is black or a melanistic bird which I have seen but never had one of them to eat, no doubt they all taste the same. Years back when I went rabbiting I once got right up close to a pure white pheasant, I did think it was a chicken as it was sitting in the hedge.

I have just made Marguerite Patten's 'Victory pie' containing minced pork, pork sausage meat, bacon, onion and several herbs and spices all baked as a raised pie with hot water paste. I made a good jelly with pigs trotters to pour into the hole in the top. Left to go completely cold it was a beautiful pie which we ate with a salad and mustard.

This leads me nicely on to my recipe of the month which is:

Tripe hot pot.

1 lb. Prepared tripe cut into small squares
salt and pepper
1 oz. Flour
2 lbs. Potatoes sliced.
1 lb. Onions sliced.
3 tomatoes sliced
stock
1 tablespoon dripping.

Roll the tripe in the seasoned flour.

Fill a greased hot pot dish with alternate layers
of vegetables and tripe, starting and finishing
with potatoes and seasoning each layer with salt
and pepper.

Pour in the stock so it comes half way up the
dish, dot with dripping over the top and cover
with a lid.

Bake in the oven for 1.1/2. hours at gas mark 5,
375F, or 190 C. taking off the lid for the last 15
mins. to brown the potatoes.

Enjoy.

Wafflings of a Villager April 2009

On the third of April come the cuckoo and the nightingale.

Spring finally gets into its stride in April as the countryside responds by taking on a mantle of vivid green, as trees and hedgerows come into leaf. Blossoms of blackthorn and damson create a spectacular sight. But with all this splendour, mid April left our forbears hungry at this time and it was known as the 'hungry gap' and it wasn't until June that some staple crops came in season to help out. It is so easy to forget this as today we have the world's production at our fingertips.
Today with early varieties, early production with the help of cloches etc. We can produce crops such as peas and broad beans, early potatoes and cabbages to fill that gap, until the main flush of foods come in. You would have come to the end of clamped potatoes around now (something that is not needed today as cold stores are used).

Soul! Soul! for a Soul cake!
I pray you good missus, a soul cake,
An apple, a pear, a plum or a cherry
Or any good thing to make us all merry
One for Peter, one for Paul,
Three for him that made us all.

So much can be sown and planted now, firstly my runner beans are sown in plastic coffee cups on the 9th. April to be planted out in May and so I should pick my first crop 9th.- 12th. July.

If you have a small plot to spare it's a good time to make and plant an asparagus bed. Plants can be bought now, and looked after, will supply you with an amazing crop of spears from April to the end of June every year for 25 years. It is so lovely to go into the garden, cut some spears, bring them in and onto griddle then smother in butter or hollandaise and eat within 6 minutes of cutting, there really is a great difference.

Time too for lifting and dividing mint, chive, etc. to increase the crop. Sowings of parsley now will provide that essential herb, all summer and autumn. French beans are ready to sow at the end of the month outdoors.

Mid month I will graft my last apple rootstock to give me a grand total of 15 fruit trees, some as espaliers on fences some as stepovers and a few as bush. So you see how you can use lap fences to effect by growing a lot of fruit. I have plum, greengage, cherry, fig, pear, several good desert apples, then there are raspberries, loganberries, strawberries and rhubarb. I lost my blueberries in tubs to vine weevil, the scourge of today.

Years ago I grew seakale and forced it to produce lovely ivory stems with a delicious flavour but alas I haven't the space to spare now.

Just a word about the Village hanging basket competition, I judge the baskets around the village on flower show week, you don't have to enter just have a good hanging basket <u>to be seen</u>

<u>from the road.</u> Well now is a good time (if you have protection) to plant up your baskets and our local lad Allen Avery will have a good variety of quality plants for sale, and good plants they are too.

24th. St Mark.

The eve of St Mark by prediction is blest,
Set therefore my hopes and my fears all to rest.
Let me know my fate, whether weal or woe
Whether my rank is to be high or low.
Whether to live single or be a bride
And the destiny my star doth provide.

I bought a piece of rolled brisket of beef at Tim's as I wanted to make some salt beef (or corned beef). The cure I use can be used for pork too, it's 6 oz. Cooking salt, ¼. Oz. Saltpetre, 1.1/2. oz brown sugar and 2 pints of water. The whole is brought up to a boil and simmered for 5 mins. then left to get cold before pouring over the meat. I use a plastic supermarket meat container with cling film over the top. This is put into the fridge for about 10 days to pickle turning occasionally. The dish I like is known as brisket pot and the beef is simmered slowly and towards the end of cooking you add whole carrots, halved leeks, a couple of onions, celery, a quartered Savoy cabbage and a faggot of herbs. Yet another meal from the past but still very tasty, fished off with some nice fluffy dumplings made from flour, suet, breadcrumbs, grated lemon zest chopped parsley, salt and pepper.

If it thunders on all fools day
It brings good crops of corn and hay.

I have been looking at a flower show report from the Gazette 1971 and given myself a good laugh. Frank Bond used to open our flower show then he would judge the fancy dress parade. The following is in black and white for all to see, it's what you may call 'stating the blooming obvious':

"Christine Berry walked away with the 50p. Fancy dress prize, but then she was the only entry," said Roy Baker Flower, show secretary.

This is part of the show that is dying down a bit now' (perhaps we had two last year). I also noted that Mrs. J.Trenchard won the tomato class as she did last year, that's consistency. And so to my recipe of the month. Chicken, cheese and tarragon pie.

CHICKEN CHEESE AND TARRAGON PIE.

2 oz. Butter
2 carrots finely diced.
8 sliced shallots
1 leek sliced finely
8oz. Button mushrooms sliced
1 oz flour
1/2 pint warm milk
1/2 Pint double cream
1 lb. Cooked chicken meat diced.
3 tbsps. Chopped fresh tarragon
2 oz. Grated cheddar cheese.
Salt and pepper.
6 oz. Short crust pastry for the base and 4 oz.
Puff pastry for the top.
1 egg for glazing.

Gently fry the carrots, shallots, leeks and
mushrooms for about 10 mins.
Add flour and cook for a further 2 mins.
Gradually add milk and cream stirring until the
sauce thickens.
Add cooked chicken, tarragon and cheese to the
sauce, season well and allow to cool.
Line a greased pie dish with the short crust.
Add chicken mixture and top off with puff
pastry, brush with egg and bake in a pre heated
oven 200c. gas mark 6 for 30 mins or until
golden on top.

Enjoy

Wafflings of a villager
May 2009.

Spud a thistle in May it will come another day
Spud a thistle in June it will come again soon
Spud a thistle in July, it will surly die

May to me is 'new potatoes', asparagus, broad beans, early carrots, and early peas, in fact almost every other day I go into the garden and pick a few peas, young broad beans, French beans, young finger carrots, new potatoes, spring onions etc and make a spring soup, very clean, light and delicious.

I am really enjoying my asparagus so much so that I saved some seed and grown on a dozen more plants so another bed is now planted which will double my crop after a couple of years. I have tomatoes planted in the greenhouse and near the end of the month I will plant out the bulk of them with heavy cropping Super Marmande which will give me a crop to make into tomato sauce which I freeze into bags for pizza topping and pasta sauces.

I may have mentioned it before but I have a pomadoro, which purees tomatoes and pushes out the seeds and skins and makes passata very quickly. My runner bean plants are to be planted the second week of May but I will be prepared if a frost is forecast with some fleece. This year I am growing an old favourite 'Kelvedon Marvel' and 'White lady'.

The fair maid who, the first of May
Goes to the fields at break of day
And washes in dew from the hawthorn tree
Will ever after handsome be.

May is a good time to plant all sorts of vegetables for a bumper harvest of fresh food. Plants like tomatoes, runner beans, peppers, chillies, lettuce, in fact so many different vegetables can be sown or planted now in containers from large fruit tins, old buckets, baths, tubs, boxes and so on. Go on have a go and give yourselves a treat.

Up merry spring and up the merry ring
For summer is acome unto day
How happy are those little birds that merrily do
sing
On the merry morning of May.

In the seventies, I ran the old 14th. Taunton Bishop's Hull now West Taunton scouts and cubs. I was myself a Bishop's Hull scout and assistant Cub Scout leader in the 50s. And what good times we had. I was a scout in the old fashioned uniform with a Mountie hat, shorts and a hazel staff. I was a patrol leader in the Chough patrol and I took it very seriously. We used to go camping at Bishop's Lydeard in the woods; it could have been thousands of miles away for we saw no one and we were in the middle of nowhere.

We made our own bread in the form of dampers, which we cooked in a Billycan. We would go into the fields and pick mushrooms, watercress, nuts and whatever we could find to eat. We made lots of mushroom soup and watercress soup, and damper bread, it was a taste I can remember today.
Our scout hut was about where the lodge to the crematorium is today. As I said, I was a leader in the old Bishop's Hull scout troop based at Galmington, so once you're in, extras add to the time you can spare and before long I was cub scout leader, scout leader, acting group scout leader, on the Somerset scouter leader training team plus all the district meetings and Trident management committee meetings it got a bit heavy going and eventually you fizzle out of steam. I was at the time too taking my Horticultural exams at Cannington College.

Button to the chin till May be in.
Nae'er cast a clout till May be out.

It is to me encouraging seeing just how much our foods are being looked at and rethought. You can now after many years buy boiling fowls, which is better tasting than the quick reared birds and are useful for casseroles, pies, coq au vin etc. although they need a longer cooking time.

218

Also at long last mutton is suddenly readily available which was a cheap staple when I was a lad. I still love the way of cooking I grew up with and my top meal is still a good steak and kidney pudding made with beef skirt and ox kidney served with dark greens like kale.

One of my all time greats from the past was mothers smoked bacon and yellow split pea soups, it stuck to you're ribs. She would take the rib bones from a flitch of smoked bacon and cook them with veg, pre soaked split yellow peas for hours and the resultant soup was so tasty. I have made some similar but never as good.

This prompts me to our recipe of the month.

Somerset Likky Pie.

1 lb. Leeks chopped
8oz. Bacon chopped
Salt and pepper.
1/2 Pint milk
2 eggs.
8 oz. Puff pastry.
2 fld. Oz. Single cream.

Mix bacon and leeks together, season and put into a saucepan.

Cover with milk, bring to boil and simmer slowly for 20 mins. Cool.

Separate the eggs.

Beat yolks together with the cream.

Whisk the whites until stiff and fold into the leeks and bacon.

Put mixture into a pie dish and cover the pie with pastry. Make a small slit in the top to allow steam to escape.

Bake in a hot oven 200c. gas mark 6 for 30 mins. or until browned.

Enjoy.

Wafflings of a Villager
June 2009.

11th. St. Barnabas

Barnabas bright Barnabas bright
The longest day and the shortest night.

What a busy time in the garden at this time of year, there's hoeing, watering, sowing, planting, and harvesting all those lovely vegetables you sowed earlier in the year. I am cutting summer 'hispi' cabbages, still eating asparagus, peas, broad beans, all sorts of salads and the new potatoes are a real treat, my garlic is being used 'green' and is fantastic. I am going to smoke some, as I love smoked garlic mash. In our changed climate it is a good idea to spray later potatoes and outdoor tomatoes with Bordeaux mixture against the dreaded blight, it can be bought at the plant centres. It is a good time to sow main crop carrots like autumn king, also long rooted beetroot for later use and storing. Plant out your spring sown cabbages, kales and Brussels sprouts and give them regular watering until established.

Calm weather in June sets all in tune.

I am planning a few bar-b-ques, as I love cooking outdoors. Sometimes I do a spontaneous Barbie but that usually ends up with a few sausages, burgers and vegetables on sticks. What I do love to do is cook a shoulder of lamb that has been marinated for hours, grilled fish like mackerel, sardines or Cornish pilchards, which they now call Cornish sardines!

A good brew to go with this is my 'Bishop's Ale'. This is made by taking 1-gallon water, 1 jar malt extract, 3 oz. Crystal malt grains, and 2oz. Of my dried fuggles hops. All is boiled for 90 mins then strained through muslin and when at blood heat, the brewers yeast is added and it ferments for a while.

Before it stops fermenting completely it is strained again and put into bottles with a half a teaspoon of sugar, crown capped and left to mature for at least three weeks. The first taste says it all, it has been praised by many a beer connoisseur and not blowing my own trumpet but leave it for 6 months and it is superb. They come beating at my door for it.
I grow my own fuggles hops and dry them off and store them in a paper sack in the loft and distribute them to my son who having tasted it now makes his own to Fathers recipe. He says that folk pay £2.00 plus for a pint like that. But mine cost's me only 15p per pint.

I do like to barbecue pork ribs that have been marinated in a sticky, hot, sweet and sour sauce for a few hours. Vegetables have their place, too, and a bamboo stick speared with mushrooms, peppers, courgettes, baby onions and tomatoes brushed with lemon, garlic and chilli oil and grilled goes well with all the meats and fish.

I bake bread rolls to mop up all the juices, which are garlic laden usually. I grow a few varieties of cherry tomatoes, some in hanging baskets that can be picked and eaten as required by friends or family as they enjoy the food. This year I have Tumbler, red cherry, sungold and Sandpoint all very tasty toms.

15th. St. Vitus

If St. Vitus day be rainy weather,
It will rain for forty days together.

As a lad I remember quite a few of the men from the village turning out to dig out the badgers from the wood at the back of the Manor house where it was reputed to be the face of a tunnel that led to the Taunton Castle. The men dug into the hill and the Jack Russel dogs were put into the digging and large metal tongues were used to catch hold of the badgers, which were dispatched quite quickly. Life in the village was sometimes quite gruesome and you just lived with it as 'that was what was done'.

I have over the years caught rabbits, shot pheasants, pigeons, ducks, fished for trout, perch pike and grayling, which are the best for eating in my opinion. I have also taken pigeons eggs, moorhen's eggs, duck eggs and pheasant's eggs for eating and enjoyed them. I remember my Father bringing home a gypsy he felt sorry for and he produced a badger ham which was beautiful to eat. He came to see us every time he passed through Taunton. I have to this day, a silk handkerchief he gave me when I was about 8 years old. He would play the guitar and sing beautifully.

A swarm of bees in June is worth a silver spoon.

My cherry tree is producing lots of cherries this year and they are ripening now so soon we will again be eating cherry clafouti, we had about 3.1/2. lbs. Last year that was its first year of cropping so we are looking forward to a good crop. I have also been making little tarts with asparagus my quail eggs and a cheese and egg custard. This leads me on to my recipe of the month.

Spicy fish cakes.

(This is not actually my recipe but Rachel
Allen's but I make them often.)

350 gms. Cooked fish (I use tinned salmon)
50 gms butter.
2 cloves garlic, crushed
125 gms. Fresh breadcrumbs.
1 egg
juice of 1 lime or 1/2 Lemon
1 tspn. Worcester sauce.
1 tspn. Dijon mustard.
1/2 to 1 tspn. Tabasco
4 spring onions chopped.
Salt and pepper.

Combine in a food processor and shape into
cakes. Chill then coat in breadcrumbs. Fry in
shallow olive oil. I serve them with summer salad
for a light lunch.

Enjoy.

Wafflings of a Villager
July 2009.

15th. St. Swithin.

St. Swithins day if thou dos't rain
For forty days it will remain
St. Swithins day if thou be fair
For forty days 'twill rain nae mair.

July at last, this means pickings of runner beans; my favourite vegetable and I hope they give good crops until the first frost (usually at the end of October.) I shall no doubt preserve some in salt as they stand up better than frozen ones in my opinion. I use an ice cream container with a wooden fitting board to weigh them down (an old chopping board cut to shape), then the ice cream top to seal.

It is so simple; you just prepare your beans for the table then to every 3 lbs. Beans you add 1 lb. of cooking salt, then as the beans are produced you just prepare and add to the box until it is filled adding the same ratio of beans to salt then start another box. To use, take out enough for your requirements and put them to soak in fresh cold water for an hour. Now cook in the same way. They will keep in salt for at least a year.

It is usually in July that I have a glut of vegetables and so I make a few batches of piccalilli using up some of the cucumbers, courgettes, beans, cauliflowers, shallots, red peppers etc. We will have a lot of tomatoes this month and I grow a good amount of basil to coincide with the glut and so I roast halved tomatoes with garlic, thyme, salt and pepper, olive oil and sometimes anchovies which when done makes a beautiful tomato sauce. Also for the freezer with onions, garlic, peppers, aubergines, courgettes and tomatoes I make a lot of ratatouille.

The raspberries are still producing, strawberries are just about finished but I am looking at about 12 beautiful 'White Marseilles' figs, it's a tree that Fred gave me a few years ago and to pick and eat a juicy white fig still warm from the sun is a real pleasure.

I have some really sweet, sweet corn and for that to be at its best needs to be taken to a boiling pot, no salt, without delay once picked and cooked for about 8 minuets. If you do it this way it will be a world away from shop bought as freshness is all. Or pick it to order, brush with melted butter and put on the barbecue.

The asparagus has now ended and we must leave the crowns to build up for next seasons crop, but I did make some last minuet asparagus, goat cheese and quail egg tartlets, as I do love that combination.

July to whom, the dog star in her train,
St. James gives oysters and St. Swithin rain.

Time in the garden to cut out fruited raspberry canes and tie in the new ones for next years crop. Take off or peg down strawberry runners to increase your strawberry bed or create a new one.

You can propagate carnations by layering them also if the weather is at all wet then spray your tomatoes and potatoes with Bordeaux mixture fortnightly against the dreaded blight. Sow some parsley now for winter use, I grow a hardy winter parsley 'Bravour' and one 12 inch pot in the cold greenhouse kept me in parsley all through the winter and spring including early summer and I did hit it hard as I use it at least once a week and often 2 or 3 times. I have had to date, a good supply of salad crops but there is still plenty of time to sow more for a continuation. Although you could say it is late in the season, you can still sow things like carrots and early peas as they have enough time to crop also beetroot.

A swarm of bees in July's not worth a butterfly.

July was when as a lad I would go into the fields with my mates to pick peas, this was usually in the fields, which are now called Waterfield Drive, Bakers close, Great Mead etc. We would take a loaf of bread from Tucks the baker on the Wellington New road and some lemonade powder and water and stay all day earning 1/6d per sack of peas and there were a lot of peas in a sack but we were "well off " by the end of the

228

day. I also picked blackcurrants up at a large house at Stonegallows for 3/- per 12 lb. basket (too much work for to little money) we thought. We would go back to my mate's house where his mother was just finishing bottling some tomatoes and fruit, as there were no freezers for most of us then and preservation was a commonplace thing in most houses whether bottled, dried or salted. It is a shame to think who will have the knowledge in the future if we don't get the younger generation involved now.

Sorry, soap box over with for now and so to my recipe of the month and as it is in season now I leave you with.

Fried sea bass on a bed of celeriac and potato
with samphire.

For each person; 1 filet of sea bass.
6 oz. Potato
4oz. Celeriac.
2 oz. Samphire.
A little butter.
Salt and pepper.
2 fld. Oz. Double cream.
A squeeze of lemon
Chervil to garnish.

Boil potatoes and celeriac until tender. Mash,
add cream and seasoning.

Meanwhile fry the filet in butter until the skin is
crisp and the fish is just cooked.

Sauté the samphire until just el dente.

Put a bed of the mash on a plate, top with the
filet of bass, add the samphire to the side of the
plate, season and garnish with a sprig of chervil.

Squeeze a lemon over the fish and serve.

Enjoy

Wafflings of a Villager
August 2009.

HARVEST HOME.

If St. Bartholomew's be fine and clear
You may have hope for a prosperous new year.

August in the garden looks so full and plentiful
and you are continually digging, picking, lifting
and cutting fruit and vegetables for the kitchen.
Some early apples are coming into season like
Beauty of Bath and Discovery etc. These are best
eaten straight off the tree, as they do not store
well. Plums and gages too are very nice to eat
straight from the tree.
 It is a good time to grease band fruit trees against
winter moths. Time to sow some turnips for a
supply of my favourite winter green tops, they
are slightly bitter and full of iron, and it was good
enough for 'Popeye'. Sow more carrots and
beetroots for early autumn use.
 Lift ripen, and store onions now. I have grown
an Italian onion with white skin called 'Cipola
tonda musona' and it looks very good. My self-
blanching celery, which was looking very good,
has suddenly got a virus and looks variegated, so
that's one failure this year. A tip worth trying for
fly is to boil a few rhubarb leaves in water and
this can be used as an organic spray against
aphids ie, green and black fly.

I did hear on the news that the interest in growing vegetables has been so great that the seed firm Thompson and Morgan has been inundated with request for vegetable seeds and has had to take on more staff to keep up with demand. How good is that? To me this is most encouraging and I applaud it.

Saturday 15th. August.
Bishop's Hull Flower Show.

Yes it's the flower show again and how good it is to see so many of the villagers supporting it. I have documentation of the show back to 1925 but believe it was running well before that date, in fact it has been going we think for certainly over a hundred years or more. It was a much grander event than now. Bishop's Hull flower show was held in the field lent by Mr. H. Quartly. Hon sec. Was C.H.Payne (I have a photo of him) at Milligan Cottage and Captain W. Mallilieu of Upcot House. It then embraced also Bradford on tone, Norton, West Buckland, Hillfarrance, Trull and Galmington. What a show. Apart from the flowers, fruit and veg. There was the band of the 5th. Battalion S.L.I. who played during the afternoon and evening. Skittling for a pig and other prizes, roundabouts, swing boats, coconut shies etc. etc. and dancing in the evening. There were also racing from the Rose Inn at Hamilton Road to the show which was about 4 miles and many shorter races. There were also horse events eg. racing, jumping and other events. Special prizes were given by Mr. G.U. Farrant, E.A.Diamond, W. Nash and sons and so on. It was certainly a date for your diary and an annual event that <u>MUST</u> be kept going. I have given over 15 years as secretary in two stages, one in the late sixties and into the seventies until I moved out of the area, then for the last ten years plus since my return to the village. We now have a small but dedicated committee. My only failure is to involve the school but alas there is no interest from the Head after several tries.

A rainy August and warm
Does harvest no harm.

Back in May at our social evening, we had a talk by Rob Waldron who is the Anglican Church Deanery rural officer and the Community liaison officer for the South West farmers. He is an organic farmer and he gave us a good insight to his work. It was most interesting and he told us of his organic beginnings into farming and we know how well he has done, winning several accolades for his produce. He started with a quiz of old country sayings and names of things long forgotten but our audience were very good at remembering and a number of us scored 9 out of 10 (it's an age thing).

It did bring us up to the question of food and how much the national average of people paid for their food. Apparently the national average amount of income paid for food was only 9%. I indicated that I must be going wrong as I reckoned that at least 50% of my income was spent on food and drink, and when I consider all the fruit and veg I grow plus the game etc. I get for free, some people live on very little.

In May (I am writing this at the end of May), we had a bar-b-q and a neighbour had one at the same time. He works at an abattoir and he bought three bags of smoked beef ribs from the works shop and he offered me a bag as he had overbought. Well I smothered them in Hoi sin sauce for a few hours and bar- b-qued them and they were the bees knees.

I also made some lamb kebabs with cumin, coriander, salt and pepper and lots of fresh mint, they were very tasty. I marinated chicken legs in a sticky tomato, brown sugar, soy, mustard, salt and pepper and grilled them on the Barbie. I made vegetable kebabs and painted them with a herb, garlic, chilli and lemon oil and also grilled them on the hot charcoals. I made some pork, apple and cider sausages and some beefburgers with herbs and onion. I then speared some sprats on sticks and grilled them too with a salad from the garden and roasted potatoes we had a very tasty meal.

In my recipe for spicy fishcakes (June issue) I am sorry to say I omitted the herbs, which should have read, Chopped parsley and chopped coriander. I hope it didn't spoil your fishcakes. I apologize profusely.

Now to this month's recipe, I was talking to a few at our coffee morning and it transpires that a few have made my brown sauce recipe and makes it often so I was asked for my tomato ketchup recipe, so here goes as it is a winner.

My tomato ketchup.

2 lbs. Tomatoes
1 lb. onions.
2 red peppers.
Oil for frying
4oz. Sugar
4 large cloves garlic crushed
1 tablespoon mustard powder
1 tbs. Paprika
2.1/2 wine glasses of wine vinegar
1/2 Teaspoon ground Allspice.
pinch powdered cloves
ground black pepper
2 teaspoons salt.

Peel and deseed toms.
Chop peppers and onions and put into a pan and
cook until soft, not brown. Add other ingredients
and cook over a low heat for around 2 hours (stir
often to avoid sticking) until a thick red sauce is
obtained, blitz and pass through a sieve and put
into hot sauce bottles or jars.
I have kept this for about a year without
sterilising.
My Brown sauce recipe was posted some time
ago now but I will include it in Septembers mag.
As the apples will be about then.

Enjoy.

Wafflings of a Villager
September 2009

September blow soft
'till the fruits be in the loft.

We will soon be thinking of picking and storing our apples and pears now. I love to have our own apples at Christmas and my favourite is an old French variety called Orleans Reinette which is a russet type with a very good flavour and it goes well with Stilton and a good port. In the garden there is still time to sow some turnip seed to give you those lovely winter turnip green tops right up until March. Manchester market is probably the best variety for this, we used to have green top stone, which was perfect, but E.E.C. regulations saw that go to the wall.

When harvesting the earlier turnips we used to cut off the crowns and plant them in shallow boxes, water and put into a dark shed then after a few weeks they would produce lovely blanched shoots and leaves which tasted beautiful.

Sow some lettuce now outside and if you can cloche them you will have large butter head lettuce in the New Year. The variety I grow is 'Valdor' and it is a very good one. Also you could sow some 'white Lisbon' winter hardy spring onions. If you haven't sown some parsley for the winter yet, do it very soon, 'Bravour' is my recommendation.

There is still time to take cuttings of your
bedding geraniums taking them about 3 inches
long and cutting just below a leaf joint and put
them around the inside of a pot of sandy compost
until rooted.

29th. St. Michael
Michaelmass day.

And when the tenants come to pay their quarters
rent
They bring some fowls at Midsummer
A dish of fish at lent
At Christmas a capon
At Michaelmass a goose
And somewhat else at New Years tide for fear
their lease fly loose.

In the wild at the moment are nuts, blackberries
all sorts of mushrooms both in the field and in the
woods. Rabbits are now in season and on the first
of October pheasants are back along with
partridge.
Back in the Spring I predicted that I would pick
runner beans as usual the ninth of July, well lo
and behold I had my first picking just as I
predicted and with broad beans, my new potatoes
and a free pheasant I had a first class meal for
free and so delicious were those beans, and well
worth waiting all that time for. It's so nice now to
go into the garden, pick some potatoes an onion
and spinach and within minuets you have (with

some curry powder) Saag Aloo. I am writing this in mid July and my sweetcorn is flowering and will soon be giving us some nice cobs of corn.
 With all the surplus of vegetables it is a good time to preserve some of it. Jams, jellies, pickles, chutneys, bottled fruits and tomatoes are nice to open in the depths of winter to remind you of a sunny warm day when you were picking them, they will come in handy too at Christmas with all those cold meats and cheeses. Next month my wife will be making the Christmas puddings and jars of mincemeat then they will mature nicely. I am constantly processing, making, curing all sorts of foods to enjoy as a change and to know what I have put into them. I have just cured two pigs cheeks as bath chaps which when boiled and covered in breadcrumbs and sliced and together with some homemade peas pudding and mustard sauce will I know go down a treat and also cold with home made piccalilli is a treat indeed.

 I did promise last month that I would again give my recipe for brown sauce which one or two people had missed.

My Brown sauce.

2 lbs. Cooking apples prepared ie. Cored and peeled weight.
1/2 lb. prunes
1 large onion.
1.1/2. pints vinegar
1 teaspoon ground ginger
1/2 Tspn.   Nutmeg
1/2 Tspn.   Allspice
1/2 Tspn.   Cayenne pepper.
1/2 Cup table salt
1 lb. dark brown sugar.
3-4 jars or bottles.

Put all fruit and veg into a pot of water to just cover. Cook until tender, strain veg. and push it through a sieve. Add vinegar, spices, salt and sugar and cook on a low heat until thick.

Pour into sterilized bottles and screw down the tops. I used to sterilize the bottles in a hot water bath at 100 degrees cent. for 20 mins and knew they would last ok for a couple of years but now I don't bother and it will still keep well for at least a year. I know a few that have made it and wouldn't buy 'Daddies' again.

And now for my recipe of the month, which I call

Gardeners soup with pesto.

I just go into the garden and pick;
a few peas, some broad beans, runner beans,
courgettes, a few tomatoes, 1 onion, a little
Tuscan black kale, a few of the very small new
potatoes, 2 sticks of celery, 1 leek, 6 or so finger
carrots
1/2 Tin haricot beans,
a small amount of fine pasta broken up,
1 desert spoon vegetable stock granules
1 tablespoon tomato puree salt and pepper to
taste.
For the pesto sea salt flakes, fresh basil, 2 garlic
cloves, some olive oil and grated parmesan
cheese.

Prepare and chop the veg.
Sweat the onions, celery and leek in a little olive
oil until soft.
Add all the other ingredients, except the pesto
ingredients, and cover well with water. Bring to
the boil then simmer until all is cooked.
Meanwhile in a pestle and mortar bash the garlic
and salt together until a puree, then add the basil
and puree that.
Add parmesan and the olive oil and mix to a
very loose puree is formed.

Put the soup into bowls and add a good desert spoon of the pesto in the middle of each and stir in.

Enjoy.

Wafflings of a Villager
October 2009.

When chestnut leaves do fall
Cotton ain't no good at all.

Time to prune your currants, gooseberries and
pear trees now cutting out old and diseased wood
before the leaves fall. It's a good time now to
plant out your spring green sand if you plant
them only 9 inches apart you can cut alternate
cabbages early leaving the others to mature to full
size, 18 inches apart. It's now I cut down the
asparagus stems and top dress the bed with
manure ready for the next crop. The berries on
some of the stems I hang on the fences as in the
depths of winter we get the blackcaps in the
garden and they love them.
In the flower garden you can increase your
herbaceous perennials by dividing them now.
Plants like michealmas daisies, phlox,
campanulas, geum, scabious, veronica etc .etc.
You can also cut off side crowns of lupin,
anchusa, oriental poppy and verbenas.
I have been eating kales for some time now, in
particular the black Tuscan kale and I am just
about to pick some sprouts and I do love them. I
am thrilled and so very thankful for the amount
and quality of the crops I have harvested this
year. I have had runner beans, broad beans,
French beans, green peas, purple podded peas,
summer cabbages, Savoy cabbages autumn

cabbage, black kale, Pentland brig kale, early
Brussels sprouts, spinach, sweet-corn, sweet
white onions, spring onions, carrots in variety,
lots of salad leaves, fennel, courgettes,
cucumbers, tomatoes, peppers, chillies,
aubergines, asparagus, beetroots, parsnips, garlic,
early potatoes, rhubarb, apples, pears, raspberries,
loganberries, gooseberries, figs, plums, cherries,
strawberries and so on, not to mention my most
important herbs; parsley, thyme, sage, bay, mint,
chives, garlic chives, marjoram, basil, rosemary,
summer savoury, tarragon, chervil, coriander, and
Greek oregano. Without these herbs I would not
feel a complete cook as they bring good flavour
to all meals.

Fresh October brings the pheasant
Then to gather nuts is pleasant.

There are some good mushrooms to be had at
this time of year, in the fields there are field
blewits or as we called them as kids, 'blue legs'
and two types of parasol which are very good to
eat. In the woods we find the hedgehog or pied de
mouton, wood blewit which is a lovely shade of
purple and very tasty, chicken of the wood and
boletus (penny bun or cep) which is my all time
favourite and just fried in olive oil, garlic and
finished off with chopped parsley and butter is a
simple but beautiful dish.

It is now I like to go out and collect some
chestnuts for the Christmas turkey stuffing's, we
used to bury them in a tin to keep for Christmas
fare and then we would as kids roast them in the
range oven.

A SHEPHERDS VERSION OF THE 23RD.
PSALM

Thur lord is me shepherd, I sharn want for
nothing. He goes afore me over thur green
dowans, an guides me by the quiet waters o' thur
Tone. He comforts me soul an leads me along
goods paths fer his names sake. Yea, though I
walks through thur shadowery ways I ain't
afeard, for his shepherds crookl guide. He'll fin a
quiet plaace fer to eat ower food arter we
overcome ower difficulties an us'll be happy.
Shurly this loveliness a'l be wi'me aul me days
till I come to thur hoome of me lord fer ever.

As it is October and a good time to make
chutneys for Christmas here is what I call 'Roy's
Christmas Chutney'. It is one I developed as a
good dark, fruity and sweet chutney which makes
7/8 jars.

My Christmas chutney.

1 pint vinegar
1 lb. dark brown sugar
1 lb. onions, processed small.
1 lb. celery   chopped very fine.
1.lb. red tomatoes chopped fine.
1 lb. cooking apples chopped fine.
1 large carrot diced very small.
1/2 lb. dated blitzed
1/2 lb. prunes blitzed.
1/2 lb. apricots blitzed.
1.1/2. teaspoons salt.
2 teaspoons black pepper ground.
2 tspns. Ground ginger.
1 tspns mixed spice
1/2 tspn. Allspice. Ground.

Put vinegar into a pan with the sugar and slowly
bring to a boil, dissolving the sugar. Add all the
other ingredients to the vinegar and stir well.
Simmer slowly until thick. Pot into sterilised jars
and label.

Enjoy

Wafflings of a Villager
November 2009.

No leaves, no birds, No vember.

The following is a paragraph I first wrote in the January 2004 magazine but I have no problem with repeating myself as this is my way of life and I still follow the ideas and the dream.

Now on these winter days when we come in from the cold, the fire is bright with a few logs I picked up whilst walking through the wood. We sit at the table to have our dinner and reflect on the year. I have started my meal with a mushroom soup and I remember picking those wild mushrooms in the woods on the Brendon Hills in the late autumn. The main course is a roasted pheasant that I shot back in October, stuffed with herbs and onions from the garden, also the vegetables, potatoes lifted in July, kale I planted in May, carrots I sowed in April and leeks I planted out in June. All this was washed down with a nice bottle of blackberry wine. To follow, apple and blackberry pie. We picked the blackberries in August and a few fallen apples. I finish with a rather nice Stilton I made back in late August and with one of my russet apples and a glass of elderberry Port we have had a free meal fit for a king. All was home produced from scratch. We can all do it to some degree and there is little that gives so much satisfaction as

providing a meal, and thinking 'that cost me
nothing and yet was so beautiful'.

Now boys with squibs and crackers play
And bonfires blaze turns night into day.

Over the early autumn I have been bottling
plums and pears, salting beans and freezing
tomato pasta sauces for the winter months. This
has been done over the generations to put a bit by
for leaner times as times could be and often were
hard. You hear tales like " my old woman can
make a meal out of anything, I've seen her take
the bones out of her corset and make a tasty
soup". Left over and stale foods were reused, ie.
stale bread became bread pudding. Milk "on the
turn" was made into a cottage style cheese and so
on, nothing was wasted.

Remember, remember the fifth of November
Gunpowder treason and plot
I see no reason why gunpowder treason
Should ever be forgot
A stick and a stake
For king Georges sake
Holla boys, holla make the town ring,
Holla boys holla boys ,God save the King.

Here is a brief glance back at the early days of
my old scout troop, 14th. Taunton Bishop's Hull,
which has just passed it's 87th. Year.

The first recorded meeting was on September 29th. 1925, under the chairmanship of the Rev. G.B.Raban, and was addressed by scoutmaster Wickenden of the Huish's school troop. Mr Raban was appointed scoutmaster with Mr. Powell as his assistant. There were 15 boys then in the troop. The group started with a President, nine vice presidents, nine committee members and five others willing to help. The longest serving founder member was the president, Capt. (later Col.) Malalieu who also acted as the chairman of the committee.

In the garden it is time to sow long pod varieties of broad bean on a sheltered site and also you can now plant your shallots. Pot up some parsley for winter use and box up some mint roots too for a winter supply. Plant young roots of horseradish to grow on for a much improved horseradish sauce. The best time now for planting small apple and pear trees in a small garden, also redcurrant and gooseberry bushes. You can also take hardwood cuttings, pushing them straight into the soil, of fruit bushes like red, black, and white currants, also gooseberries etc. for new plants to set out next autumn.

Time now to give my recipe of the month.

Pheasant braised with Celery.

1 pheasant.
Salt and pepper.
1/2 Pint of stock
3 rashers of unsmoked bacon in strips.
a knob of butter.
1 glass of port
1 head of celery
1 egg yolk
1 onion chopped.
1/2 Pint of double cream

Brown the pheasant and onions in the butter then put it breast side down in an ovenproof dish with the onions.

Add bacon to a saucepan with the port and stock, bring to a boil then pour over the pheasant. Cover the dish with foil and put into the oven for 30 mins at 180.c. gas 4.

Finely slice the celery then remove the pheasant from the oven, turn it right side up in the pot and pack in and around with the celery. Season well. Return to the oven for a further 30 mins. or so. Now beat together the egg yolk and cream and mix with the cooking liquor and thicken on a gentle heat to create a rich sauce.

Serve with potatoes Anna and a green vegetable. Rich and tasty.

Enjoy.

Wafflings of a villager
December 2009.

21st. St Thomas
St. Thomas Grey, St. Thomas Grey,
The longest night and the shortest day.

Well here we are at my favourite time,
Christmas. Ever since a lad and to this day I have
absolutely loved Christmas. It's not receiving
presents but the whole feeling that folk are more
pleasurable and warmer. It must be the giving
and love we send out, being returned but
whatever it is I am sure it's people feeling the
warmth in one another. We look back over our
youth at the good times we had as families and
we feel comfort and security.

At Christmas play and make good cheer
For Christmas comes but once a year.

I also love Christmas carols and play them from
morn 'til night and at times I can see my wife
pulling her hair out. I do love the old ones like
Coventry carol, In Dolce Jubilo, In the bleak mid
winter and so on. I remember as a lad on
Christmas morning going to the hospital
clutching my little dart board and darts to show
my father what I had been given for Christmas
and I couldn't understand why he had tears in his
eyes, I thought he must be hurting bad. Despite
some not so good times I still love it.

251

Just a word about our climatic peculiarities, in October I was picking strawberries again and despite September being the driest month since 2006 we still had good harvest of late raspberries, courgettes, cabbages etc. My apples are still good in store and my russets are at last in season. I really do look forward to them, they cannot be bought but such a wonderful flavour. I have planted my shallots and garlic and they are on course for a fine crop. I shall now sow my onion seeds to plant out later. I have some mixed salad leaves in the cold greenhouse border together with some spring onions and chervil.

Something a gardener was expected to do expected to do was to make decorative wreaths etc. for the front door and I still make mine every year. I just use a wire ring and tie in conifer to make a base, into this I wire holly sprigs, berries, variegated ivy, and some silk Christmas roses. A few fir cones, red ribbons in coils and there you are a £20. wreath for a few pence. I also have made swags of holly, ivy etc. to decorate the chimney breast together with a few baubles makes a fine decoration. Also above the pictures I decorate fir, holly, ivy baubles and red ribbon as we like the natural look. We have a real Christmas tree that smells of pine together with the aroma of oranges, almonds and nuts is all part of Christmas in our home.

December in the garden doesn't sound too exiting but there are a few things to do for instance shallots are traditionally planted on the shortest day Dec. 21st. and harvested on the longest day June 21st. Large onions are sown in heat in December to be planted out later to make those very large onions. I occasionally grow one tomato plant in a pot in the conservatory for some very early tomatoes and those are sown now. Any digging can be done now weather permitting. It's a good time to put lime on the ground that brassicas are going to be grown on and the winter weather will take this into the ground. As we seem to have more winds these days it's good practice to stake your Brussels sprout plants, if they rock in the wind they are likely to make the sprouts blow open into useless crops. Some of the shorter varieties like Peer Gynt are not affected so much.

In the kitchen there is much to do for me as I like to make the stuffing's for the turkey and freeze also make mini chipolata sausages and wrap them in home made bacon for a garnish. I always make a terrine and often an ox tongue and a ham and if we expect many more, a raised game pie. One thing I like to make is parmiers which are heart shaped puff pastry biscuits filled with anchovy and parmesan also parma ham and cheese. These go by the bucket full as does home made cheese grissini.

On New Years Eve my youngest grandson Thomas Aleksander Baker will be three years old. Happy birthday Thomas. He is teaching me

Serbian but he knows to speak to grandpa in English.

It's time now for my last recipe of the year so lets not talk Paxo here is the real deal:

My chestnut stuffing for turkey.
Sage and onion for goose or duck

Tin of unsweetened chestnut puree.
3 oz cooked chestnuts broken up.
1 large onion chopped and sautéed.
8 oz. Breadcrumbs.
15-20 sage leaves
1 large onion chopped and sautéed.
5 stems parsley Chopped.
Salt and pepper.
3 rashers of bacon fried and chopped
a little water to moisten.
1.1/2. oz shredded suet.

Mix all together and pop into freezer until needed.
Combine in a large bowl and mix well.
Add enough water to bring
together. This can be made ahead of time and frozen to save last minute work.

Apple prune and brandy sauce for goose.

Macerate 6 oz. Prunes in Armagnac or brandy for 12 hours. Core peel and slice 2 cooking apples, mix with the prunes add salt and pepper and place in the cavity of the goose, (put the sage and onion stuffing in the neck cavity).

Roast the bird and the residual sauce goes very well with the goose.

Wishing you all a very happy, healthy and peaceful Christmas.

Best wishes, Roy Baker.

WAFFLINGS
OF
A
VILLAGER
2010

Wafflings of a villager, January 2010.

I would like to wish you all a very happy, healthy and prosperous New Year.

As the days lengthen.
So does the cold strengthen.

Well here we are in 2010. I have written 2 pages in the magazine every month for nearly six years now. I did consider having a break but a few have told me to keep going so I will try to do so. I did wonder if readers could help me by sending in letters (questions) on gardening, cooking, preparing foods and processing foods. It would help to bulk out my copy to Bob. My e.mail address is artybaker @ tesco. net
January in the garden sees me sowing some vegetable seeds. I sow some tomatoes, peppers, chillies and aubergines now, as well as summer cabbage (Hispi) early Brussels sprouts, and some lettuce. It is surprising how easy and convenient it is to grow and harvest a few vegetables. They can be grown in pots, containers etc. on a patio if a vegetable plot is out of the question. It is surprising just how much can be grown in a small space. I have a comparatively small garden and yet I haven't had to buy any cabbages, kales, sprouts, and sprouting etc. at all. I crop tomatoes from early June until late December, likewise aubergines peppers and chillies. There are always roots of some sort or another; I am currently

enjoying parsnips, carrots, beetroots, and Jerusalem artichokes plus the much smaller Chinese artichokes. One veg that I have missed for years now are leeks, they have failed miserably so this year I must get on top of them. My pears (Concorde) have produced for the first time, 15 large pears in all and were superb, we have only a few left. Other fruit in store is my apples 'Orleans Reinette' and a few 'Crispin', 'Kidds Orange red' and Holstein Cox'. A couple of apples I grafted last year should provide a taste of things to come this year, one of these is an old cider apple called 'Sweet Morgan' and it is a lovely apple to eat with a good Cheddar. Talking of which, there is a very strong and flavourful Cheddar called 'Black bomber' and my wife brought me back some from Snowdonia where it is made. We have found it in Butchers row in Barnstable and now in Taunton in the ' Olive tree' in Bridge street. Anyone who likes a jaw jolting Cheddar should certainly try some.

Over the Christmas I have enjoyed some lovely food. Tim comes up trumps with his beautiful turkeys, a good smoked gammon ham which seemed never ending, endless Stilton to keep the Port flowing, smoked pheasant pate and lots of cheese, anchovy and olive biscuits. I have made a New Years resolution to make bread on a more regular basis. I love sourdough bread and once you start, it must be made regularly to keep the sourdough going. Just a useless piece of information; the American cowboy of yesteryear was known as a sour belly because they carried a lump of sourdough starter in a bag around their waist to make their bread on cattle drives.

5th. Twelfth Night.

Twelfth night is sometimes called Twelfth day eve, old Christmas eve or the eve of Epiphany. After the change from the old to the new style, certain districts continued as far as possible, to keep their Christmas on 6th. January and to wassail their apple trees on 17th. January, sometimes called old Twelfth night.

Health to thee good apple tree,
Whence thou may'st bud and whence thou
may'st blow
And when thou may'st have apples enow
Hats full, caps full. Three Bushel bags full
And my pockets full too.

This is the time for my recipe of the month and the start of the year. We need fresh new tips of the dandelion, or I do use spinach for;

Nettle gnocchi with Dolcelatte sauce

7 ozs. Nettle tips
1.1/2. lbs. Floury potatoes peeled and cubed.
7 ozs. Plain flour
1 large egg. Plus salt and pepper.
<u>Dolcelatte sauce.</u>
3,1/2 ozs. Dolcelatte cheese cut into small cubes.
3.1/2 fld. Ozs. Milk.
2 ozs. Butter.
To serve, 2 ozs. Grated parmesan.

Cook the nettles in boiling salted water for 10 mins. then drain and squeeze out all the liquid. Cook the potatoes until tender then drain and mash to a puree.
Put the mash on to a work surface and mix in the flour.
Liquidise the nettles with the egg and season. Add this to the potato mix and knead to a soft dough.
On a well floured surface roll out pieces of dough into little sausage shapes ¾ inch in diameter and 1.1/2. inches long. Dust with flour.
Using a well floured fork, take one at a time and roll it down over the prongs to form a pattern that resembles little ridged shells.
Leave to rest on a cloth. Next combine the Dolcelatte and milk and process together.
Melt butter and milk and cheese and allow to melt over a low heat.

Bring a pot of salted water to boil. Add gnocci.
When they rise to the surface they are ready.
Drain and add the sauce immediately. Sprinkle
with parmesan cheese and some black pepper,
serve hot.

Enjoy.

Wafflings of a Villager February 2010

2nd. Candlemas

If Candlemas be fair and bright,
Winter will have another fight,
If on Candlemas day it be shower and rain,
Winter is gone and will not come again.

February, the bright and sunny month is here, pheasants, mallard and partridge are now out of season but you may if you are quick, be able to buy the last few fresh ones, although rabbit and venison is still available. Now is the time for the beautiful pink forced rhubarb, which is indeed a treat not to be missed. Bacon has no seasonality today but in the past, pigs were a crucial part of the annual cycle in Britain where bacon, the longest lasting and therefore most treasured product of the beast. Pig meat may indeed be valuable, but it spoils easily, so quick work and careful techniques are required to get most out of it. The blood, guts and offal were dealt with first, creating delicacies such as black puddings, sausages, chitterlings and faggots, all of which helped to eke out for a few weeks the bits of the pig that would otherwise go off too quickly. Other parts in particular the sides and haunches were preserved by salting, (and may be smoked as well) to keep for much longer as ham and bacon. The latter in a large side or "flitch", would be hung from the ceiling or high in the fireplace

262

to smoke. Smoke acts as a deterrent to insects, forms an antiseptic seal on the meats surface and of course, imparts an extra note to the flavour. The bacon and hams were much prized by the cottagers at it kept them in bacon and lard for a whole year.

Shrove Tuesday

Pit pat the pans hot
And I be come a shroving;
Cast the net before the fish,
Something is better nor nothing,
A piece of bread, a piece of cheese,
A piece of apple dumpling;
Up with the kettle and down with the pan,
Give me a penny and I'll be gone
Give me another for my little brother,
And we'll run home to father and mother.

February is the month when my Victorian Parma Violets flower and they were used by my Mother to decorate my birthday cake with after crystallizing them. It's strange how a little thing like a violet evokes such strong and pleasant memories. I went into a friends house the other day and the smell that hit me was similar to an Irish stew and straight away I was transported to a wartime British restaurant that was in the 'Victorian rooms' in the centre of Taunton, now alas pulled down. Mother took me there when our school dinners at St.John's school failed during the winter of 1947. You had to purchase Bakelite tokens. Then went along the line asking for the meat of the day and handed over a red token, next was the veg and a green token etc. etc. They cooked very good meals but it was cases of 'have what's going', it might be rabbit pie or corned beef hash or a stew probably of whale meat.

If you marry in lent
You will live to repent.

In the garden now I plant my broad beans. I am not a lover of the autumn sown bean 'Aquadulce' as it is a white seeded bean and hasn't the taste of a good green seeded bean. My beans although sown in February and not October / November time mature only a few weeks behind them so not a lot is gained but the flavour is so much better. I have a variety from the 60s. and 70.s that is unattainable now called 'Dobies rentpayer', it is so good that between a few of us, we keep the variety going. Another variety I grow is 'Masterpiece green long pod' and it is easily available. It amuses me to hear top chefs telling people to skin the beans after cooking so they are tender. It is obvious to a keen gardener that this is unnecessary and only because they are left too long on the plant to get old. I harvest mine when they are young and not when the scars from the pods are black and the skins leathery. Broad beans and sweetcorn are the only vegetable I freeze as I do think they freeze well.

The sun peeps through the window pane
Which childern mark wi' laughing eye

Blackbirds are now starting to pair up so spring isn't far away. We have had our visits from the Blackcaps who come every winter and they are a sight to see. My hazel and wild primroses are on full bloom now and as far as I am concerned, that's spring. It is time now for my recipe of the month and as we are still chilly and wanting comfort food, I leave you with;

Braised lamb shanks with canellini beans.

2 lamb shanks
1 can canellini beans drained
4 tomatoes
1 stick celery
2 tbsps. Olive oil.
2 garlic cloves, chopped.
1 large onion peeled and cut into 8/ths. through the root.
1 large carrot chopped into 2" chunks.
15 fld. Oz. Red wine.
1 fresh bay leaf.
2 tbsps. Fresh rosemary bruised then chopped.
Salt and black pepper.
A lidded flameproof casserole (4 pints).

Chop toms roughly, cut celery into 2" chunks,

Pre heat the oven to gas mark 1, 140 c. Heat the oil in the casserole to high, season shanks and when the oil is hot, brown on all sides.

Remove from the pan when brown and add celery, onions, and carrots and brown as well for approx. 6 mins. Add garlic and stir in, cook for 1 min. then add the beans.

Next add the tomatoes, wine, bay leaf, chopped rosemary and some seasoning.

Finally place the lamb shanks on top and when brought to a simmer, cover with lid and transfer the casserole to the oven to braise very slowly for 3 hours. Serve garnished with a rosemary sprig.

Enjoy.

Wafflings of a Villager, March 2010

1ˢᵗ. St. David's day

Upon St. David's Day
Put oats and barley in the clay.

March, and in the garden we have lots to do. It is the start of much sowing and planting for good crops of vegetables later. I sow lettuce, beetroots, peas, Brussels sprouts, spring onions, more broad beans, watercress in pans, cabbage, celery and later in the month, courgettes and cucumbers sown under glass. Plant out the seedling onions you sowed at Christmas time. After chitting your early potatoes these can now be planted and if you can cover with fleece or cloches, you will get them a little earlier. It's a good time now to prune your rose trees as pruning them regularly you will keep them young with good fresh wood on them. Under glass sow some dwarf French beans in 8inch pots, 6 beans to a pot and you will have some early beans and they do crop very well. In the garden I am still cropping young shoots of my kales and these are the best of all as the young budding shoots are like very tender sprouting. I usually grow a kale called 'Hungry gap' and this comes into cropping just around the end of the month when there is little else, ie. 'The Hungry Gap', but alas this year I ran out of space, so I will have a hungry gap of my own.

'As a sweet pledge of spring, the little lambs
Bleat in the varied weather' round their dams.'

Seasonality means so much to me and I believe
to live with the seasons and eat foods that are at
their best then is the only way. I am a bit pedantic
about it but nothing but your own first strawberry
or picking a sun warmed ripe fig or cherry from
the tree is totally magic. I also love now to go to
my little patch of wild garlic or Ransom's and
pick some leaves for a salad etc. is absolutely
lovely. It also makes a good soup with some
watercress and a poached bantams egg on top.
The first tomato in season lifts the soul, after all
those useless, acidic tomatoes that are available
in the stores. The first of the seasons crab after
not having one for a while is a sublime treat. I
believe if we buy food that is in season we would
appreciate the best tastes of our food and enjoy
them a lot more. Seakale, a Victorian vegetable is
in season now and beautiful it is too, it's a
vegetable you cannot buy generally. It's a root
that is forced and blanched like the best rhubarb.
I think I may grow some again as I haven't grown
it for years. I see Unwins catalogue does it as 5
thongs for £14.95 for a mid March delivery and
like asparagus and artichokes it's a perennial and
once established you have it for years.

March comes in like an adders head
And goes out like a peacock's tail.

Back in January I was making warming casseroles with oxtail, stewing beef etc. and also several curries for the freezer in case of bad weather, and indeed we did have some bad weather. I made an authentic Indian rice dish from a lady called Vindhiya, known in the family as Vindhiya from India, and the rice is made with rice, onions, cashew nuts, garlic, bay, star anise, mace, cumin seeds, garam masala, biriani masala, green chillies, grated nutmeg and coconut milk. It is a very special rice that you could eat on it's own as a dish. I made lamb Rogan Josh, chicken korma, chicken and cashew nut curry and also a quite hot Beef Rendang curry from Malaysia, which is a beauty. Now we are thinking of lighter spring like meals with fresh tastes like; Sheep's cheese and spinach tart (yes sheep's cheese has a season) with a gratin of purple sprouting with garlic, chilli, anchovy and cream, which is also at it's best now.

Gratin of purple sprouting.

Peel and thinly slice 4 garlic cloves, deseed and chop 2 dried chillies. Put olive oil in a heavy pan and add the garlic, chillies and 6-8 anchovy filets. Fry until garlic is golden then add a splash of white wine or masala ,boil for a few seconds then add 400 mls. Double cream. Bring to a simmer and turn down heat and cook until reduced by one third. Blanch the purple sprouting in boiling water for 1 minute, drain and allow to steam dry.

Lay the broccoli in an oven proof dish, pour over the cream sauce and scatter with 100 gms. Grated parmesan. Bake at 190.degrees gas mark 5 for 10-12 mins. until golden and bubbling. A good recipe too for kale.

Spinach and sheep's cheese tart.

Pre bake a short crust pastry tart shell. Blanch about 750 gms. Spinach in boiling water for 2 mins. Remove and refresh in iced water. Drain, squeeze out excess water then roughly chop. Finely chop a large onion and put into a pan with a good knob of butter, a pinch of chilli flakes and the finely chopped cloves of garlic. Soften in the butter then add to the chopped spinach and season with lemon juice, salt and pepper and nutmeg. Spoon the mixture into the pastry case and top with 100gms. Grated hard goats cheese, such as Berkswell. Combine 2 eggs with 200mls. Double cream and season to taste. Pour over the spinach mixture and bake at 180 degrees c, gas mark 4 for 30 mins. or until just set. Serve at room temperature.

Enjoy.

Wafflings of a Villager April 2010.

2nd. Good Friday.

The first of April some do say,
Is set aside for All Fools Day,
But why the people call it so,
Nor I nor they themselves do know.
(Poor Robin's Almanac for 1760).

April, and spring has arrived, and what a glorious time of the year it is, with spring flowers in the hedgerows, birds nesting, singing, buds bursting and a whole new look about the countryside. I love to see young rabbits on the grass verges at Silk mills road, running about without a care in the world until they try to cross the road. When you look into the hedges you can see several hop plants and I often wonder if they are a few of the hops that were grown in the village as they were years ago for the Malt house and Starkey Knight and Ford's brewery.
I grow a hop called 'Fuggles' and I use it to brew my own beer. I do everything from scratch so there are no kits for me and it makes a very good bitter. I call it 'Bishop's Ale' as we called the village as kids. I read on my deeds that I must not brew beer on my land, it was a clause put in place by the Hanburys who lived in the big house at Mountway. This was placed in the 1800s. but I don't envisage making beer at quantities more

271

than I can manage to drink myself with the help
of my family.

The blossoms open one by one
And sunny hours beguile

This is the month when I start to cut my
asparagus and the first cutting is rushed into the
kitchen, steamed and anointed with butter or
Hollandaise and it really takes some beating.
These crowns reproduce regularly every few days
until I stop cutting at the end of June.
In the wild there are two very good mushrooms
to be had now, namely the 'Morel' and the 'St.
George's' mushrooms and both are very good.
Watercress is out there now along with beautiful
young shoots of Hogweed.
I am too very fond of hop shoots and these can
be gathered and cooked just like asparagus.
Primroses were picked years ago to adorn
'simnel' cake. New potatoes from the channel
islands ie. Jersey Royals are to be had now as a
pre taste to our own freshly dug 'New potatoes'.
Brown cock crab is coming into season and how I
look forward to that.

24th. St. Mark.

The eve of St. Mark by prediction is blest,
Set therefore my hopes and my fears all at rest,
Let me know my fate, whether weal or woe,
Whether my rank is to be high or low,
Whether to live single or to be a bride,
And the destiny my star doth provide.

In the garden now we can prepare and plant an asparagus bed and that will last us for around 25 years and provide lots of tasty asparagus. On the ninth I sow my runner beans in pots in a cold greenhouse to give me beans from 9th. July until the first frosts. It is time to plant out my summer cabbages (hispi). More peas go in now and I am growing a tall old variety 'Alderman' and it can be picked over a long period. The tomatoes I sowed back in February can now be planted in the cold greenhouse together with aubergines, peppers and chillies. I will also now sow my courgettes and cucumbers to plant out later next month. All manner of seeds etc. can be planted now like beet, onion, carrots, chard, spinach and always-small sowings of salad leaves.

Sow French beans outside toward the end of the month. Sow broccoli and kohl rabi. The second week is time to graft my apple trees and I usually do cleft grafting. Years ago Easter was the time when everyone took to the garden to dig, plant and sow, as it was a holiday and land workers had little time to garden at home but the produce was much needed to keep body and soul together.

If it thunders on All fools day
It brings good crops of corn and hay.

The trout fishing season is now open and I loved to go to Clatworthy and bring home 5 (total bag) of nice fresh trout. It was Fred who some years ago taught me to cast a fly, on the lawns of the Frank Bond Centre, he was a good teacher. He also taught me how to tie flies and so I became proficient in fly tying. When you have tied a fly and you land your first trout on it there is a sense of achievement. I once caught the best brown trout for the whole season weighing four and a half pounds and had my name in the Gazette, (large head). I often smoked some and made smoked trout pate or made trout gravadlax using Fred's recipe, and talking of recipes, I leave you with my recipe of the month.

A nice fish dish for Good Friday.

Sautéed Squid with Greek salad.

12 oz. Prepared small squid
2 Tblsp. Olive oil.
2 sprigs fresh thyme
1 garlic clove finely grated.
A pinch of dried chilli flakes
A good pinch of sea salt.

Plenty of ground black pepper.

For the Greek salad- 2 salad tomatoes, skinned, seeded and cut into half inch cubes, 3 oz. Cucumber cut into half inch pieces, 2 oz. Feta cheese into cubes, 1 small red onion finely chopped, 8 black olives, 1/2 tblsp. Chopped fresh fennel herb or dill.
Dressing. 2 Tblsp. Extra virgin olive oil, ½. Tbspn. Red wine vinegar.

Put all the salad ingredients in a bowl and mix together gently. Whisk together all the dressing ingredients, season and stir into the salad.
Cut the body of the squid into rings, the fins into strips and the tentacles into three. Heat olive oil and thyme in a pan and when hot add squid and fry for about 2 1/2 Minutes , add garlic, chilli flakes, salt and pepper and then toss for about a minute.
Serve immediately with the Greek salad. Very nice.

Enjoy.

Wafflings of a Villager, May 2010.

1st. May Day.

Up merry spring and up the merry ring
For summer is a come unto day
How happy are those little birds that do sing
On the merry morning of May.

May means, fresh garden peas, new potatoes,
young broad beans, asparagus, young finger
carrots, salads, wild garlic, watercress and
seakale if you can find it in fact a wealth of
young fresh vegetables that are clean flavoured
and beautiful as a pre summer feast. Morels and
St.Georges mushrooms are still about now, and
what a treat when you find them, also pignuts
which I love, they are a similar taste to chestnuts
and quite easy to identify and dig up. For the
good of your heart, pulse and blood pressure
problems, infuse 2 teaspoons of fresh hawthorn
flowers and leaves in a warmed pot with 600mls.
Of boiling water and steep for 10 mins. before
pouring.
 Spider crabs are in season now and are
overlooked by most, so ours are sent out to the
continent. They have lots of white meat on them
and do a very good crab linguini. Broom buds are
nice too smell and taste of coconut. Hop shoots or
hogweed shoots steamed and anointed with butter
or hollandaise sauce is so good. Watercress and

wild garlic make a terrific soup with a poached
egg on top and all free for the gathering.

The fair maid who, the first of May
Goes to the fields at break of day
And washes in dew from the hawthorn tree
Will ever after handsome be.

In the garden now there is much to do.
Towards the end of the month you can plant out
your tomato plants after hardening them off. Also
sow outside some runner beans, we used to say
10th. May is kidney bean day as if you sow them
then it takes three weeks to germinate and show
above ground so this is the end of May and
frost's should be gone. Sow out of doors too
ridge cucumbers, marrows, sweet corn. Plant out
Brussels sprouts, celery seedlings and leeks. I
always think that in May you need more than
ever to keep the hoe moving between the rows of
vegetables. If you haven't done it yet plant up
those hanging baskets etc. for the flower show
Village hanging basket competition. Our local
plant centre, which sponsors the class, on the Silk
Mills road produces some of the very best plants
I have seen. My tomatoes are flowering and I
look forward to some fine tasty tomatoes soon. I
sent off for some 'cow cabbage' seeds, as a lad
we used to come home with a cow cabbage we
could hardly carry but they were quite sweet, we
were offered them to feed our rabbits but I cut
grass and herbage for them so we ate the cow

cabbages. I have sent for some horseradish roots, as it is so much better than the horseradish sauce that is available. We used to dig up some along a lane when we were kids and it was grated and vinegar, mustard and cream added to make a beautiful horseradish sauce to go with a nice fore rib of beef. I have also planted some seakale thongs so in the future we have yet another delight to look forward to.

Mist in May, heat in June
Makes the harvest come right soon.

You would hope we have a reasonable summer this year as for the last 2 summers I have had only three barbecues as we had much rain and winds. I love to cook and eat out of doors; I think it is because of my Scouting background. To this end I have two brick built barbecues and a cast iron chimnea so there is plenty of room to cook. I also use my hot smoker to hot smoke sardines, sprats, trout, sausages and small meat filets. I have hot smoked quail eggs, mushrooms and even cheese. It brings another dimension to barbecued food. We had an outside area (patio) covered with polycarbonate so we can stay dry. There is also coloured lights surrounding the area with a central light and these are all underneath my grapevines so we can eat and pluck grapes like a Roman emperor. I do believe a barbecue meal needs as much planning as a full dinner party or it degenerates into black burgers, sausages etc. As we are thinking food it reminds me that it is time for my recipe of the month.

Marinated herrings.

4 herrings, cleaned and soaked in salt water for 1 hour. (I take out the main bone.)
4 oz. Caster sugar
8 fluid oz. Malt or cider vinegar.
1 bay leaf
1 tablespoon pickling spices.

Heat to boiling point sugar and vinegar, bay leaf and pickling spices, then set aside to cool.
Drain the herrings, cut into 1-1/2. inch pieces, dry well and set aside.
Put the herrings in the cooled vinegar and set aside to marinate for 3-4 hours.
Remove and arrange in a serving dish. Garnish with wedges of tomato and sprigs of fresh dill.
Serve with salad and brown bread and butter.

Enjoy.

Wafflings of a villager June 2010

Barnabas bright, Barnabas bright
The longest day and the shortest night

June is here and so midsummer is upon us. It is lovely to sit outside and have your meals in the warm evenings with a glass of wine. Weather permitting we have breakfast, lunch and dinner sat under the grapevine with the coloured lights on until bedtime. I love a barbeque and if it is a nice day we will light up and cook an al fresco meal. I have a chimnea (It might be worth mentioning that on two occasions I have mentioned the chimnea and Bob has corrected my copy as chimney, not so Bob, it is a 'Chimnea', a cast iron wood fired oven.) and it will cook a shoulder of lamb over wood beautifully.

The produce from the garden comes into play with new potatoes, peas, broad beans, and asparagus etc. etc. so we have them in season and very fresh, and one bite tells you just how good they are. I do rant on a bit about growing some vegetables and when I get through to some of my friends and they try it, they suddenly realise just what they are missing. I have just got our neighbour to rip up half of his lawn to have a go.

Some sow a few late runner beans so the season is assured until the frost. I still have some of last year's salted beans in good condition but I do look forward to fresh ones next month. I have been enjoying, straight from the garden, asparagus, broad beans, peas, hispi cabbage, new potatoes, radish and salads. My first tomatoes are with me now and what a delight they are. I have enjoyed rhubarb, strawberries, also a few gooseberries and now raspberries and loganberries.

> *At eve last midsummer no sleep I sought*
> *But to the field a bag of hempseed brought*
> *I scattered round the seed on every side*
> *Then three times, in a trembling accent cried,*
> *This hempseed with my virgin hand I sow,*
> *Who shall my true love be, the crop shall show*
> *I straight looked back and. If my eyes spoke truth*
> *With his keen scythe, behind me came the youth.*
> *'The spell' John Gay, 1714.*

There is still work to do in the garden to keep all the produce coming, like spraying your late potatoes and outdoor tomatoes against blight, which we have had the last couple of years. I use Bordeaux mixture, obtainable from garden centres etc. Sow maincrop carrots now for the winter use also long rooted beetroots. You can still plant out spring-sown cabbages and leeks. Sow garden Swedes and earth up potatoes. In the flower garden, prune your early flowering shrubs like weigela, spirea and mock orange or philadelphus. Restrict your sweet peas to one or two shoots per plant for larger flowers and tie in or ring and remove the tendrils for nice straight stems. I have planted a few gypsophilla plants to pick and ad to bunches of sweet peas for indoors. There is still time to sow pots of basil, dill, etc. as herbs are good to have and essential in our house. I also sow Thai basil, which has that essential Thai flavour. The best job in the garden of all is in the vegetable garden now picking and lifting the vegetables as required and enjoying them. Finally keep the Dutch hoe moving.

Now summer is in flower and natures hum,
Is never silent round her sultry bloom.

Back in the forties at Bishop's Hull school, in June we often went by bus up on the hills to Cothlestone, West Bagborough, Wills neck and on occasion to Dunkery Beacon. I have a photo of a few of us on Dunkery beacon which my old school master Mr. Winter gave me only twelve years ago, he was then in his nineties. He ruled us with a rod of iron but was always fair and most pupils thought the world of him. He could rattle off the names of the whole of my class and we are talking just one class he took 60 odd years earlier. He always showed interest in any project or pastime you were interested in. He also taught my son who is now 42, years later.

15th. St. Vitus.

If St. Vitus' day be rainy weather
It will rain for forty days together.

There are some seasonal treats to be had in June. Elderflower is blossoming and if you pick some on a bright sunny day when the scent is high, it will make some refreshing lemonade or champagne. I like to have some flower heads and dip them into batter and fry, then drizzle over some honey and what a treat they are. Fresh, green or wet garlic is around now and it is welcomed as it is an entirely different veg. Compared to the dried bulbs. It's milder, sweeter and less pungent. It can be eaten raw in salads or roasted as a vegetable. It is also an antibacterial and anti- fungal and also acts against the clotting of blood. What goes better with fish soup than 'aioli' (garlic mayonnaise).

New season peas are available and you have to go into the garden to pick your own to know what a pleasure it is to have young sweet and flavourful peas. Real old fashioned new season lamb is too a flavour apart from so called lamb at other times. Mackerel too are right in season now and they have to be very fresh and are very good with omega three oils. I have either mackerel, salmon or herrings once a week for that reason. Samphire is now available and is nice as a side vegetable with fish, it can be bought or foraged for free. There is some at Porlock bay around the flats. I have pickled it and it makes a welcome change. With beautiful fresh seasonal vegetables etc.

It is time for my recipe of the month.

New Season lamb sweetbreads with broad beans and bacon in a cream sauce with boiled new potatoes.

1 lb. lamb sweetbreads, (see Tim).
1 1/2. lbs broad beans
2 rashers bacon roughly chopped.
1 small onion, chopped
5 tablespoons double cream.
New potatoes.
Put potatoes on to boil, place onion in a pan with half butter and half olive oil and sauté until cooked but not browned.
Add bacon and sweetbreads.
Boil briefly until just cooked, your broad beans, add all together until just cooked.
Season with salt and pepper and add cream.
Serve at once with the new potatoes.
A little Dijon mustard can be added with the cream if liked.

Enjoy.

Wafflings of a Villager, July 2010.

15th. St. Swithin

St. Swithin's day, if thou dost rain,
For forty days it will remain,
St. Swithin's day, if thou be fair,
For forty days 'twill rain nae mare.

I would like to start my wafflings by saying that we had a family Baptism in Church on the 30th. May 2010. It was the baptism of my Great, great Niece Ellie Iris Wilson. Her parents Nick and Emma, grand parents Debbie and Tony and her great grandfather John Wilson were very proud. John's late wife Iris, my sister, would have been so very proud of her great granddaughter. Another one of the family to be connected to the village. Afterwards we all were treated to a carvery meal at the Old Inn and it was good to catch up with relatives.

July is here and a season of plenty in the garden, with new potatoes, peas, new carrots, runner beans, dwarf beans, summer cabbages, sweet corn, tomatoes, chillies, peppers, cucumbers, courgettes and so on. We really are spoilt for choice now. All those hours put into producing the veg has paid off a hundredfold. We are also picking cherries, strawberries and raspberries. Things we have planted to crop later is in and growing away like sprouts, kales, sprouting broccoli, winter and autumn cabbages and cauliflowers. A versatile veg I am growing too is Swiss chard 'bright lights', the leaves can be cooked as spinach and the multi coloured stems can be braised or gratinated as a tasty dish. Pak choy, an oriental cabbage type also easy to grow and is good in Chinese style stir fries, it goes well with a dish of mine where a bass or similar is steamed with ginger, chilli and spring onions, when cooked it is knapped with oyster sauce and boiling oil poured over to crackle and crisp. So you can see it is well worth trying and growing the less usual vegetables sometimes. It is possible and I have successfully grown, ginger and lemon grass to maturity. I had problems with my leeks for the last two years but this year I have a very good looking row of leeks called 'elephant', so here's hoping. Shallots, globe artichokes, kohlrabi, fennel is also around now with fruits like black and red currants also blueberries.

> *Cut your thistles before St. John,*
> *You will have two instead of one.*

In the garden now despite the gluts, are jobs to be done, for instance, cut out the old fruited canes from summer raspberries and start layering strawberry runners to increase you plants. Make a start on summer pruning your apple and pear trees but leave the leaders until autumn. Sow parsley for winter and early spring use now, also cut back parsley going to seed. Continue to spray your outdoor tomatoes and main crop potatoes with Bordeaux mixture against blight. Mulch runner beans to keep in the moisture. Sow spring cabbage towards the end of the month. Now is the time to 'bud' roses. I remember this from a lad when Mr. Rugg, who lived in the lower half of the now Constitutional club, taught me how to bud roses on his allotment 'on' the Silk Mills road. Lift, divide and replant irises and sow hollyhock, antirrhinum, gaillardia anchusa and foxgloves on a border to transplant out later.

Daughter of pastoral smells and sights
And sultry days and dewy nights.

In the wild, horseradish is prized as the best sauce for beef and smoked fish, sea holly roots can be fried as chips . Salsify roots are lovely first boiled then skinned and fried in butter or gratinated. Burdock roots are nice just roasted. Samphire is succulent and grows in the salt marshes around the coast (see June mag. For samphire at Porlock) also seakale which also grows on the coast in the shingle. Pig nuts are still around and are very tasty to eat, also known as earth nuts. Barberry berries (berberis vulgaris) can be made into jam or a nice tart jelly. Use wild gooseberries and raspberries as normal. Wild strawberries too are small but well worth the picking as the taste is superb. Field mushrooms will be out there soon and an early morning forage and return in time to fry a nice couple of rashers of smoked bacon. Wild mushrooms giving off that black juice with a very fresh egg and some bread to mop up the gravy is as good as it gets. I well remember years ago when an acquaintance thought I had missed quite a few good-sized mushrooms came and taunted me with them. I told him I left them as they weren't good to eat as they gave most people terrific stomachache and sickness. Well he would not take my word for it as he was convinced I was telling him a yarn. Well he was off work for three days as the good looking mushrooms, I knew as yellow stainers worked on him, just a scrape on the skin turned bright yellow in seconds. You really have to be absolutely certain when harvesting from the wild. I did attend several fungus forays and learnt from a few experts just, which was edible and good to eat. One or two mushrooms I eat can play some people up but with those types I was advised to eat a small piece to see if I had a reaction, then increase the amount next time but only one ever upset me enough to leave it out of my basket, it was the 'cloud agaric'. After the Cep, porcini or penny bun, hedgehog and chanterelle, my favourites are the two parasols (which can upset some people), chicken of the wood, beefsteak fungus which are both bracket fungus and the two blewits both field and wood which is a beautiful violet colour and very tasty. Thinking of the taste of these mushrooms is making me think of food and so to my recipe of the month.

Crab Cakes.

1lb. fresh white crab meat,
1 egg well beaten.
1 teaspoon Dijon mustard.
2 teaspoons horseradish.
2 teaspoons Worcester sauce.
8 spring onions. Finely chopped.
3 tablespoons chopped fresh parsley.
3 oz. Fresh breadcrumbs
1 tablespoons cream.

4 oz. Dry breadcrumbs to coat
1 1/2 oz. Butter.
Salt and black pepper.

Mix all the top ingredients together and season.
Form into round flat cakes.
Coat with the dry breadcrumbs and fry in the
butter for about 3 mins. each side until golden.

Serve with lemon wedges and chopped dill.

Very nice with salad and a chilled glass of
Muscadet.

Enjoy.

Wafflings of a Villager August 2010.

Harvest home.

Harvest approaches with it's bustling day
The wheat turns brown and the barley bleaches
grey.

Where is this year gone, it seems only weeks ago
that we were putting away our trestle tables for
the flower show, but here we are again. A lot of
work goes into producing a flower show
annually. There is the hall to book, judges,
sponsors to write to asking for their support,
posters to print, prize cards, exhibitors cards,
schedules to alter etc, I have to do my rounds
asking the local businesses for raffle prizes,
arrange who is doing what on the day. Prompting
our village stalwarts of the need of their most
valuable help. Tim our butcher does much to help
with schedules, entry forms for children and the
now annual scarecrow competition. The village-
hanging basket has to be judged as does the
scarecrows, not to mention the show itself. I have
judged the flowers, fruit and vegetables for the
last 30 odd years certainly and so I obviously
cannot show any of these but I can show
handicrafts and cooking. (I once won the cup for
best home craft with a large plaited loaf of
bread.) It has been a great and pleasant
accomplishment to see the show take off and
enlarge over the last 11 years since we took over

the running of it. We are now as big as we can get with the space available to us. Could I take this opportunity to say 'keep it up Bishop's Hull' we are sure it has been running for at least 100 years and we hope to see it continue from here on. We have had to increase the cost of entries from 50p. to £1.00 for as many entries as you like and the entry to the show has increased also to £1.00, children under 12 free. I hope this will go some way to balance out the increasing cost of running a show ie. Hall charges, insurance, printing, cup engraving etc. etc.

A man should live within his harvest.

 In the garden now an old trick was to cut down the tops of broad beans to encourage a second crop, this works well if a good watering is applied with a feed. Sow turnip seed like a green top variety to supply winter greens later, and very tasty they are too. Sow carrots, globe beetroots and winter spinach now to lengthen the seasons. Plant out winter greens, kales and sprouting broccoli. Lift and store shallots also feed leeks with a liquid manure. Time to pot up hyacinths, narcissus and daffs. Gather early apples when ripe and wrap in oiled paper. Store any apples and pears as ready. Put grease bands on fruit trees against winter moth. Cut down all fruited wood on loganberries. Sever your new strawberry runners now and replant in a new bed. Keep picking vegetables as available. Remove some leaves from tomatoes in the greenhouse or outside to let the sunlight ripen them. We have had some lovely crops to enjoy, I am thinking in particular to my favourite runner beans, tomatoes, new potatoes, asparagus, broad beans, peas, peppers, and chillies etc. My sweetcorn is just about ready and are worth growing as the freshness is tasted like you wouldn't believe against shop bought.

Dry August and warm, does harvest no harm.

A friend of mine went fishing off Porlock bay, and brought me home 2 beautiful black Bream. I descaled one and filleted it and I have just eaten half of it within 24hours of being caught I battered it and deep fried it until golden and made some tartare sauce, its so easy and so much better than Tescos etc. The fish was honestly the best I have eaten in many a year, so very fresh and flavourful, it went down well with new potatoes and freshly picked peas, what a treat and cost's nothing. We also had a very good bar-be-que with my daughter, son in law and 2 grandsons James and Dominic. I made some very nice lamb kebabs from a breast of lamb, boned and de fatted then minced finely and seasoned with salt, pepper, cumin, coriander and loads of fresh chopped mint. A little finely minced onion was added and 1 egg. This was moulded around a pre watered bamboo skewer and cooked on the Barbie. Next I made a sticky brown sugar and tomato marinade for some pork ribs. I made beef burgers next with minced Aberdeen Angus beef a little onion, salt pepper fresh thyme and parsley with a touch of chilli flakes and 1 egg. These were very tender and moist and not a bit 'black'. With a salad from the garden and new roast garlic and rosemary potatoes, and curried quail eggs we had a very good meal.

A pot without bacon is like a sermon without St. Augustine.

Now for my recipe of the month.

Barbequed breast of lamb.

Breast of lamb on the bone.
3 oranges
4 fld. Oz. Mild chilli sauce.
2 level tablespoons clear honey.
1 teaspoon salt
1/2 level teaspoon pepper
a good dash of Worcester sauce.

Cut lamb into portions, grate 1 tablespoon zest and 4 tablespoons juice from 1 orange.
Mix zest and juice with chilli sauce, honey, salt, pepper and Worcester sauce.
Put the lamb in a roasting tin and pour the mixture over the top of each portion.
Bake at 180.c. Mark 4. for 2-2.1/2, hours until tender, basting with the sauce occasionally.

293

Slice the remaining oranges, 15 mins before the end of cooking time, add the orange slices to the portions of lamb to heat through.

A nice dish to serve with a barbeque.

Enjoy.

Wafflings of a Villager September 2010

28th. September Michaelmas eve.

*And when the tenants come to pay their quarters
rent,
They bring some fowls at midsummer, a dish of
fish at lent,
At Christmas, a capon, at Michaelmas a goose,
And somewhat else at New Years tide for fear
their lease fly's loose.*

I am going to repeat a passage that I wrote in
August 2006. I make no apology for it as it is as
relevant now as it was when I first wrote it.
Back in March Sue wrote about bringing back
real cooking and having a 'be bothered to cook
month'. Did anyone give it a try? Well I would
like to try again but not for a month, but always.
If we look back, we can remember a family
gathering around the table for meals, and this was
where solutions to problems were resolved, ideas
shared, (along with secrets), hopes and dreams
talked over, worries shared; we were in fact a
family unit that could talk to one another. One
hears so many times that dinner is eaten from a
tray in front of ''the box''. Where have we gone
wrong? It was whilst giving a talk to the 'Good
Companions' on artisan cooking and processing
that whilst trying samples of my processed foods
like breads, butter, cheese, sausages, brawn,
bacon, beers, wines etc. etc. that several said to

me "'that's what food used to taste like" and
"'why cant we buy stuff like that" and "'My
mother used to make this and that". It was then I
realised that generally not many did home
processing or indeed with the younger generation
very little home cooking from scratch. We see
recipe cards at supermarkets, take 8 oz. T---o
finest marinated salmon filets a sai-----ys pre
baked flan case etc. etc. and you can cook a meal
to remember. Mrs. Beeton's recipe would start
'first catch your fish'. Well I hope I have got you
thinking.
    It really is so much more wholesome to cook
from scratch as you can see exactly what you are
buying and you also know what you will be
putting into it, ie. No M.S.G. , aspertain, and not
bucket loads of salt, sugars, gums, emulsifiers, E
this and E that. It must be better for us and our
children so come on lets get 'Proper' cooking.

On Michaelmas day
The Devil puts his feet on blackberries
(Or worse)

    The garden now has lots of crops to enjoy like
cabbages, runner beans, French beans, sweet
corn, courgettes tomatoes, aubergines, peppers,
chillies, salads, beetroots, leeks, some apples but
all the berries are over now except the late
raspberries, but what a season we have had. My
cherry tree gave us a very good crop, as did the
raspberries, strawberries, loganberries, and I have

planted 2 blackberries and a Tay berry. My horseradish plants look good and I can't wait to make some real horseradish sauce. September also means that my Brussels sprouts won't be long now, and I do look forward to those. That's what seasonality is all about, one crop goes out of season and another comes in.

Thus harvest ends it's busy reign
And leaves the fields their peace again.

   Mushrooms are out there now and don't they taste good. Some of the woodland types will appear soon and they are well worth collecting as the 'Penny bun', blewits, 'Shaggy ink cap' 'Giant puff balls' (will feed dozens) and 'Parasols' are beautiful. I just like to sauté them in butter, garlic and parsley and I sometimes add cream, it's a dish made in heaven.
 Rabbits are in the butchers shop now and next month sees the new pheasant season, and what a treat they are. Tim will no doubt have some for sale. Blackberries are free, and are still to be had and with a few windfall apples make a beautiful pie or tart. Hazel nuts too are out there free for the picking, so you could come back from a forage with mushrooms, nuts, and blackberries.

 Well talking food again brings me on to my recipe for the month.
   Fish Timbales with creamy red pepper sauce.

1 lb. white fish, skinned and boned.
3 small egg whites.
15 fld. Oz. Double cream.
2 large courgettes.
2 large carrots.
3 red peppers.
A little cream for the sauce.
Salt and pepper.
2 tablespoons fresh herbs, chopped, eg. Parsley, chives tarragon.

Process the fish, egg whites and herbs in a blender until a smooth puree is obtained. Using a wooden spoon gradually work in the cream into the fish puree. Now put the fish 'mousse' in the fridge.

Meanwhile slice lengthwise, with a vegetable peeler, the carrot and courgettes. Blanch them in boiling water for 2 minuets then refresh in ice cold water and drain.

Next butter 6 small ramekins and from the centre outwards, lay alternate strips of carrot and courgette to line the ramekins, leaving the vegetables trailing over the edge.

Now fill pots with the fish mouse and lay the overhanging vegetable strips on top to cover. Sit the pots in a Bain Marie (tray of hot water), in the pre heated oven 180c. gas mark 4 for approximately 20 mins.

To make the sauce, roast red peppers until blackening then remove skin, seeds and blitz in a

blender with a little stock. Season, put into a pan and add cream and reheat. T
 Turn out ramekins on a plate and surround with pepper sauce.
 Serve as a starter or a fish course.

Enjoy.

Wafflings of a Villager October 2010.

A good October and a good blast,
To blow the hog, acorn and mast.

Here we are, the start of the pheasant season,
also partridge, mallard, snipe, goose, grouse,
hare, wood pigeon and woodcock. For those who
don't use game can I tell you, that you are
missing out big time? Wild meat has roamed or
flown free and is usually low in fat, in fact
venison is down as a super food because of it's
leanness. Look how much more healthy we were
during and after the war, eating rabbits and
anything in the way of game that came our way.
Add to that all the mushrooms and other wild
food that is available to us from now on until
Christmas and you see just how good life can be.
As I write this (August 18th.) with a glut of
tomatoes, I have processed 5 pints of tomato
passata in my Italian Pomadoro (tomato press), I
just turn the handle and tomato juice and pulp
goes down one Shute and the seeds and skins go
down another, magic. There is a host of
vegetables out there now and in season, including
fennel, salsify and scorzonera, which are some of
my favourite roots. Also in season now are some
of our nuts like chestnuts, walnuts, and hazelnuts.
There is much fruit too at this time so do try
some of these in season. Quince when ripe, smell
just beautiful and make a superb pink jelly. One
of my favourite fish is in season from now on,

that is the sprat, which I love just plain fried in flour, smoked or soused.

> *Fresh October brings the pheasant*
> *Then to gather nuts is pleasant.*

  Something I used to begin my talks on Artisan food producing and processing with, was a paragraph that sums me up absolutely and though I have written it before, I make no apologies for repeating it. All this has been true to my way of life as I have on very many occasions done just this.

 Now on these winter days when we come in from the cold, the fire is bright with logs we picked up on our walk through the woods. We sit at the table to have our dinner, and reflect on the year. I have started my meal with a wild mushroom soup and I remember picking those mushrooms up on the Brendon Hills in the autumn. The main course is a roasted, stuffed pheasant (free food) that I shot back in November, stuffed with onions and herbs from the garden, also the vegetables, potatoes lifted in July, kale I planted in May, carrots I sowed in April and leeks I planted in June, all washed down with a nice bottle of blackberry wine. To follow, an apple and blackberry pie. We picked the blackberries in August. A very nice Stilton cheese I made back in early August, which is now well matured and goes well with a nice russet apple and a bottle of elderberry port. It is a far cry from a burger from Mc.Donalds but it is my belief that we must grow, buy and use local foods, in season like we did years ago and to encourage the younger generation to cook 'Real Food' or we will lose the knowledge to cook like our forefathers. I have always enjoyed growing, gathering, fishing, rabbiting and 'procuring' game. Living in the past is what my family call it, that is foraging, bartering and generally obtaining wild and free food.

Hey- how for Hallow E' en
When all the witches are to be seen,
Some in black and some in green,
Hey- how for Hallow E' en
(Denham tracts, 1895).

In the garden now there are jobs to be done, vegetables that are cleared for store or have come to an end can have ground dug roughly to allow the winters weathers to break it up, also lime can be applied to ground destined for next years greens and Brussels etc. and allow the winters rain s to get it into the soil. It's a good time to divide michaelmas daisies, phlox, geum, scabious, campanulas, helenium etc., also cut off side crowns from lupins, oriental poppies and verbascum and replant. Prune currant bushes, gooseberries and pear trees. A good time too for preparing ground for fruit and bushes. You can now sow mustard, rape or tares for green manuring. Set out spring cabbages and cut down asparagus ferns. Sow lettuce in seed boxes and place in a cold frame. It is a good time to save vegetable seeds, like tomatoes, onions, leeks, ridge cucumbers, peas and beans. You can firstly save your favourite varieties also save a lot of money, particularly when you think of a packet of tomato seeds at anything around £2.00 a packet, and they will stay viable for certainly 10 years if saved correctly. I have this year saved an old American heritage variety 'Oregon Spring' against the odds as I last saved seed dated October 1995, and found only 1 seed left which I sowed and it germinated, so when it was a few inches high I cut off the tip and rooted it in water so I ended up with two plants and now I have saved fresh seed which will last another 10 years at least.

I would like to take this opportunity to say thank you to the villagers who turned out in showers to support your flower show. I considered it was a great success, long may it continue. Thanks too to the tea ladies and to Kenny without whom we would struggle.

It is time now for my recipe of the month. Ideal for your Halloween party, pumpkin, (seasonal). It's a Nigella based dish with a bit of juggling from me.

Keralan fish curry with squash.

1 lb. firm white fish
salt
1 teaspoon turmeric
1 tablespoon veg. Oil
1 medium onion sliced into half moons.
1 long red chilli sliced.
2 cm. Piece fresh ginger into batons.
A pinch of ground cumin.
200 mls. Coconut milk, (1/2. tin.)
1/2 tablespoon tamarind paste.
A little fish stock.

Cut fish into bite sized pieces and rub with a
little salt and turmeric. In a pan heat the oil and
soften the onions without browning them. Add
the sliced chillies add the ginger batons along
with the remaining turmeric and cumin and fry
for a few mins. Pour tin of coconut milk into
measuring jug and add 1 tablespoon tamarind
paste and the fish stock, using boiling water,
bring the liquid up to the half litre mark. Pour
into the pan, stirring it in to make the delicate
curry sauce. Taste and add more tamarind if you
like it.
 When you are ready to eat, add the fish to the hot
sauce and heat for a few minuets until cooked
through but still tender. Add cubes of roasted
butternut squash or any orange pumpkin. Serve
with lemon rice.
Enjoy.

Wafflings of a Villager November 2010

Remember remember the fifth of November
Gunpowder treason and plot
I see no reason why gunpowder treason
Should ever be forgot
A stick and a stake for King George's sake
Holla boys holla boys make the town ring
Holla boys holla boys God save the King

As I write this (Sept 1st) I have just had for breakfast a large helping of Field Mushrooms and how good they were with egg and bacon. It was a gift from a neighbour who knows of my liking for all things wild and free, and they are poles apart from cultivated ones. Most of the fields of my youth for mushrooming are now housing estates so I must look for pastures new for my foraging.

November brings all game like Rabbits, Hares, Pheasants, Partridge, duck, venison, woodcock and pigeon. All very good meat and so versatile to use. I do use quite a lot.

Pheasants are widely available as more is shot than used at this time which is, to my mind, a sad state of affairs. I was brought up to believe that if you took a wild animal for food you should use it all and respect what you have. Even with farmed food I am still an advocate of nose to tail eating and using up the entire animal.

Take your average pig: from the head I make brawn; Bath chaps; crispy pigs ears and the legs are good just roasted or cured into hams. The shoulder makes good pate, also together with some of the belly I make my sausages, chorizo and salami. The belly of pork goes for sausages, streaky bacon and also stuffed and rolled for slow roasting. The loins make good back bacon or chops and will roast very well. Tenderloin is good for medallions which cook quickly. I use some belly pork together with the pigs liver, heart, lights and melts to make my faggots. Kidneys are just fried. This leaves the actual guts, which when cleaned thoroughly and plaited become chitterlings, which are very nice boiled then fried. This really just leaves the trotters and tail which are simmered for around 3 hours and eaten hot. The brain can be steamed in butter and milk or egged, then into breadcrumbs and fried – very nice. Thus the whole animal is used.

11th St. Martin.
It is the day of Martilmasse
Cuppes of ale should freely passe
What though wynter has begunne
To push downe the summer sunne

In the garden now it is a good time to dig over and lime vacant plots; plant apple, pear and berry bushes like gooseberry etc; take cuttings of fruit bushes like red and blackcurrants and gooseberries; force seakale and steak large Brussels Sprouts. Also it is a good time to: plant shallots and sow long-pod varieties of broad beans; keep picking winter greens to provide a larger supply; prune grape-vines and pot up parsley and mint roots for a winter supply in a cold frame or greenhouse.

I like to keep an eye on my stored apples and pears as it's said that pears are only ripe for a day and remembering last years crop of fifteen, I wouldn't like to miss a single one. They were so juicy, it was a pear which Fred grafted and gave me, called 'Concorde'. Years ago we would lift some runner bean roots now and box them up to provide plants a little earlier next year, but this practice is seldom used these days.

This night we came a-souling good nature to find
And we hope you will remember it is soul-caking
time
Christmas is coming and the goose is getting fat
Please put a penny in the old man's hat
If you haven't a penny, a ha'penny will do
If you haven't a ha'penny a farthing will do
If you haven't a farthing, God bless you.

Next years Flower Show has been arranged for Saturday 13th August 2011. The judges have been booked so you have ten months to make, grow, cook, photograph etc. Our photo classes are 'British seaside' and 'Somerset landmarks' so go on and have a go. We decided too that our Scarecrow competition will have a theme: 'Traditional Scarecrow' i.e. Worzel Gummidge-like.

There is still time to make piccalilli, pickles and chutneys for Christmas and they do go down well with cold meats and cheeses etc. I am trying a couple of new ones to me this year, one involving beetroots, onions, apple and orange. The other one is tomatoes, onions, fennel bulb, apples, celery and chilli. I will also make some beer now for Christmas as two months maturing makes a good pint.

It is now time for my recipe of the month and as we are into winter cold weather I leave you with a warming dish of comfort food. A bonfire night treat for a party that will keep you warm.

Pea and Ham Soup with crusty bread
(Serves 6)

Olive oil
2 Sticks of Celery – trimmed and diced
2 chopped onions
1/2 tsp dried thyme and 1/2 tsp dried marjoram
500grms dried yellow split-peas soaked overnight
250grm piece of smoked ham hock
1 and 1/2 litres of chicken stock
Salt and pepper to taste

Put some oil in the pan and sweat with celery, onions and dried herbs for 10 mins.
Add the peas and ham, pour in the stock and bring to a boil.

Reduce to a gentle simmer over a low heat (don't add the salt yet or the peas will stay hard) until the peas are soft.

Take out the ham and chop and shred it up. Blitz the soup or mash if you prefer more texture, stir in the shredded ham and season with salt and pepper.

Now make some crusty bread with: 1lb strong white flour; 1 1/2 oz of butter; 1sachet of dried yeast; 1 1/2 tsp of salt and 10 fluid oz tepid water.

Mix well and knead until elastic.

Put into an oiled poly-bag to prove until doubled in size.

Break into 8 rolls or a loaf and leave to prove again.

Place into a pre-heated oven (Gas 6, 200c) for 15 minutes for rolls or 30 minutes for a loaf.

Enjoy

Wafflings of a Villager December 2010.

At Christmas play and make good cheer,
For Christmas comes but once a year.

Well here we are again Christmas time and my
favourite time of the year. Ever since a lad I have
loved it. It's not having oceans of presents, as I
never got a lot as a child for the war was on and
money for a family of 6 didn't go too far. We
always had good food for Christmas and all other
times as we kept geese, chickens and ducks so
there was usually meat for the table. We as kids
would collect and squirrel away some chestnuts
etc. for Christmas. Before Bishop's Hull school I
went to St. Johns church school and we always
had a marvellous time there and would act out the
Christmas story (I was always a shepherd) and
have marionette shows, then carols with father
Jennings and Father Saunders. I love carols and
to this day start playing them from early
November much to the annoyance of my wife. I
used to get 6 shiny ha'pennies from my only
grandparent; she used to shine them up with
brasso. So with a few crayons, lead soldiers and
an orange we were about there. We were happy
with our lot then and still am now.

21st. St. Thomas, 'didymus'

St. Thomas Grey, St. Thomas Grey,
The longest night and the shortest day.

310

I have for the past seven years written 2 pages per month in the magazine which equals 8 pages of an exercise book which equals 672 pages of text in total which is converted into 168 printed pages. Recipes total at least 90 which is enough for a cookery book for my family. I do feel that I have got stale and repetitive so have decided to have a break and just do an occasional page.

I do thank you all for your comments and interest in some of my articles and hope you got something out of them over the years. I remember some time ago when I had a nasty virus in my computer and two months articles changed suddenly into Russian text. I still haven't converted it back to English yet, but I want to collate all my wafflings into book form to pass on to my grandchildren to show what granddad got up to.

It is good to remember some of the village characters and also to remember their look on life in the village, people like the Smith Brothers, Charlie, Walter and Bert who were all so involved with the flower show as their father was before them and all in their 90s. There was May Day who worked tirelessly for village life. Aunty Mary Drew who as far back as I can remember baked cakes and scones etc. for our scout parties and all sorts of fund raising events. What a true trooper she was. Stan and Dot who did more than their bit over many years, Fred Yeandle did an enormous amount for the village and villagers.

Lillian Southwood could run teas single handed with her eyes closed and often wasn't even asked. They all had stories to tell and could remember events etc. that showed village life in an informative way. I don't think we will see there like again but I do hope to document some of their observations in the future.

If the sun shines through the apple trees on Christmas day,
When Autumn comes they will a load of fruit display.

We think of Christmastime as a dull time of the year with foods, but there are the sprouts, kales, cabbages, broccoli; then roots Jerusalem artichokes, carrots, Swedes, turnips, celeriac, parsnips and salsify or scorzonera. We have too, onions, leeks, celery, and chicory. Sea bass is in season as well as whiting, mussels and brown crab hens. With game we have a number at our disposal: goose, mallard, partridge, pheasant, snipe, woodcock, pigeon not to mention grouse, hare and rabbits. A few of these are not easy to find but they are out there to be had. My favourite late apple Orleans Reinette is right in season now so do try it. Robin Small who started the farmers market in the town is at Charleton Orchards and he grows it as his favourite too. None better with a late bottled ruby port and a hunk of mature Stilton. Cheese. Some of these apples are polls apart from the supermarket favourites that have a long shelf life and no flavour. One other I now grow to be eaten straight off the tree in September is 'Bakers Delicious' the texture, taste and juice is sublime. Another is 'Kidds orange red' and even the windfalls will keep well but the taste is superb.

If on New years day the wind blows south,
It betokenith warmth and growth,
If west much milk and fish in the sea,
If north, cold and storms there will be,
If west the trees will bear much fruit,
If north east then flee it, man and beast.

There are some things to do in the garden even now. Winter prune apple trees and winter spray them with tar oil wash. Prepare new ground, prick the lawn over with a fork and brush in builders sand. Protect Christmas roses by placing moss around them. Pinch out the tops of wallflowers that are growing too tall. Buy your seed potatoes for early planting and leave to chit on trays. Prepare a warm border for early vegetable growing. It's time now for my final recipe of the month and one for the Christmas period:

Rudolph pie.

2 lbs. Venison finely cubed.
1 cup red wine
1 teaspoon salt,
4 slices streaky bacon chopped
2 medium onions, chopped
4 oz. Mushrooms chopped
2 oz. Peppers, chopped
1/2 pint chicken stock.
Black pepper, bouquet garni and a bay leaf.

Place venison in a casserole ,pour wine over, stir
and leave to marinate for a few hours.

Fry the chopped bacon and onions for a few
mins.

Drain the venison and brown in the same pan
and return to casserole.

Heat the reserved red wine marinade in another
pan with the stock. When boiling add peppers
and bouquet garni and pour into the casserole.
Stir well and cook in a slow oven for 2 hours.

When cooked remove herbs and transfer to a pie
dish.

Cover with well mashed potato to which has
been added some grated cheese.

Put back into oven until brown and bubbling.

Serve with sprouts, chestnuts and roast parsnips.

Enjoy and keep cooking.

Wishing you all a very merry and healthy
Christmas.

Roy Baker.

.

OCCASIONAL WAFFLINGS

2011 - 2013

Occasional Wafflings of a villager
October 2011.

The season of mists and mellow fruitfulness.

I did promise that I would write an occasional
article for the magazine. I did write for 7 years
and now nothing for 9 months and how quickly it
has flown by.

The three ages of Countryman
*At heart we are all countrymen, it's just that
some have lost their roots And need reminding of
days when, grandfathers walked in greener boots,
In childhood leads life's dance as green ways
beg us to explore
And every season brings romance but last's for
evermore.
In middle age we drift away in search of gold
and more and more.
And ever in our better days see country fields as
factory floor.
But in old age romance returns to haunt the
heart of yesteryear
And then the countryman soon yearns for fields
he once held dear.*

I do love this time of year as we certainly are
spoilt with the variety of foods available to us
now. We have a large variety of home grown
apples and how good are they against those from
around the world. We do grow the very best in

the world in our climate. There is a wealth of game available to us now like rabbits, pheasants, partridge, wild duck, venison, hare, pigeon and even wild boar. What fantastic meats they are and there to be enjoyed in season. We also have a wealth of vegetables, some roots such as potatoes, carrots, Swedes, turnips, onions, scorzonera, beets, Jerusalem artichokes and Chinese artichokes. Greens like Brussels sprouts, cabbage, kale, broccoli, cauliflowers etc. And we still have runner beans, courgettes, tomatoes, cucumbers, peppers, chillies and aubergines.

Nature now spread around in dreamy hue
A pall to cover all that Summer knew.

There is always something to do in the garden and at this time of year I like to clear and dig any ground in readiness for future crops. Every year I try to plant more perennial crops and to that end, this year I have bought some new strawberry plants to make a new bed. These things need to be done if you are to get the best crops continually as the old plants get tired and diseased, so fruit less vigorously. I have kept a few of the runners from my old plants which were a variety called 'Elsanta', which has been a favourite of mine for 20 years, but now I bought some 'Cambridge Favourite', 'Alice', 'Monterrey', 'Symphony', and 'Calypso', two of which are everbearers so a long season is on the cards.

My horseradish thongs I planted last year can now be lifted and used to make some superb horseradish sauce. I have grafted a few more apples and have two more varieties now namely 'Sunset' and 'Ashmeads Kernel'. I have also put on to a stronger rootstock 'Dr.Kidds orange red' and 'Bakers Delicious' and they are growing away well. It is good to have perennial food plants as you know when they can be harvested. I have also planted some globe artichokes and seakale in the herbaceous borders as they will look quite ornamental and make fantastic eating. I have too grown lots of perennial flowers to thicken up the flower garden, lupins, aquilegia 'makana giants', foxgloves (upward facing), phlox, delphiniums and hollyhocks.

> *Now that it is October,*
> *Don thy woolly smock.*

In the wild now there is a host of wild mushrooms to be had, as long as you are sure of the ones you are taking. The Lawyers wig or shaggy ink cap is unmistakable and as long as you pick them before they go black and produce the ink they are beautiful. Giant puffballs are also unmistakable. There is the chicken of the woods which is an orange/ yellow bracket fungus found on trees which is beautiful. The penny bun, cep or porcini is one of the best and can be found in the woods from now on. The purple wood blewit

319

and the purple legged field blewit are both very mushroomy and a little goes a long way. The hedgehog or Hydnum repandum is another easy one to find and identify. You can find chestnuts etc. out there now and I usually get mine now and make my chestnut stuffing for the turkey and freeze it. Still out there are bullaces (wild plums), sloes and some crab apples which make a wonderful jelly, as does quince.

I bought some sausage seasonings from an Italian colleague in Bolton, it was his 'extra special barbecue seasonings' and I made some sausages for our Barbie, but my wife found them too hot and spicy, my daughter took a deep breath, and even my son in law said "wow that was something else''.

Well I will finish as always with a recipe and as we have so much game to enjoy, I give you:

Oriental poached pheasant with star anise and chilli.

1.1/2. pints chicken stock
1/2 Teaspoon Sichuan peppercorns
1/2   "   dried chilli flakes
1/2   "   black peppercorns
1/2   "   fennel seeds
2 or 3 cloves.
2 star anise
1" piece of cinnamon stick
2 garlic cloves sliced.
1 oven ready pheasant
1 teaspoon salt.
To finish the broth,
4 oz. Fresh udon noodles
2 heads of bok or pak choy cut in half
lenghthways through the stem
1/2 inch piece of fresh ginger peeled and cut into
julienne
1 medium hot chilli halved, seeded and sliced
into thin strips
2 spring onions halved and finely shredded
Some coriander leaves.

Put the stock and all the aromatic flavourings
into a pan, bring to the boil, lower the pheasant in
barely covering. Add salt and bring back to a
simmer 15- 20 mins. until just cooked.
Remove pheasant and place on a board.

Strain the stock to pan and bring back to a boil, add udon noodles, bok choy, ginger and chilli and simmer for 4 mins. Cut up pheasant legs and breast, divide the noodles and bok choy between 2 deep plates, top with the pheasant then ladle over the hot broth and sprinkle with the spring onions and coriander leaves.

I love this so enjoy.

Roy Baker.

Occasional wafflings of a villager
March 2013

1ˢᵗ march, St David's Day.

Well here we are 2012 and how the years click by as we get older. Older we may be but what a fulfilling life we have had, with so much to do and to occupy our minds and spirits and hopefully lots still to do. In gardening we go through the seasons, planning, sowing, planting, maintaining and finally reaping the rewards of our labours with so much beautiful fruit and vegetables to cook with.

In these times of hardship more and more people are returning to growing some vegetables and for me it is so good to see. I know of young mothers who are taking on allotments and making a good job of them. Some of the older, wiser men allotment holders are giving them the benefits of their knowledge, so in the future their families will be better for it.

I have already made a start with sowing seeds like early Brussels sprouts, tomatoes, chillies, summer cabbage Hispi, shallots, garlic and broad beans. I grow Masterpiece green seeded and an old one not available now but a friend and I are keeping a stock of it and both grow it every year, it is a bean called 'Dobies Rentpayer' and has to be the best tasting bean ever.

My first early potatoes "Accent' are now ready
to plant as they are well sprouted. They have
been hard to find and last year I had to send away
for them and the postage was quite a price. I have
saved a few for a row or two.

Time to get your apple trees pruned now and any
roses that need rejuvenating by cutting back quite
hard to encourage new, young and vigorous
growth. I am looking forward this year to my
globe artichokes producing a nice crop. With the
seasons altering now I picked several
strawberries at the end of November and even
into December, and to pick strawberries whilst
the primroses are flowering is something of a
quirk of nature.

Even through the winter months I am harvesting
cabbages, kales, Brussels sprouts, and soon
purple sprouting broccoli which I love anointed
with a dressing containing garlic, oil, vinegar and
anchovies. A vinaigrette made in heaven.

I have just last month lifted some roots of my
horseradish and what a big difference that makes
to a fine fore rib of beef. I grate the root and put it
into jars with a little English mustard powder,
salt, a touch of sugar and white wine vinegar. The
jars go into the store cupboard then whenever I
need horseradish sauce I only have to take out a
few teaspoons and add a little cream, and it is so
far removed from the jars of sauce with its turnip
and preservative, colours, etc. You even taste
'real horseradish'.

I have started receiving a weekly organic vegetable box from Stoneage organics' through at least the winter months as we miss the fresh tasty vegetables through the winter although I get some things I already have in the garden but I consider it is a good £7.00's worth. The days have gone when I had three allotments to provide all my fruit and vegetables and I have to make the best of my garden to fulfill my needs, I am still eating my own apples from store and how good were they at Christmas with stilton and port.

March comes in with an adder's head and goes out with a peacock's tail.

I have through this magazine met a couple from Kent who wrote an article sometime ago who lived in the village during and just after the war with relatives. Well I recognized a couple of his comments on relatives in the town and village so he came down to see his relative and wanted to meet up, so Editor Bob and Margaret who know him arranged a meeting at their House. As we met and talked over a nice buffet (thank you Margaret), we realized we were in fact related through my great grandfather – so now I have another relative.

Another couple I have 'met' on the Internet asked Bob if anyone knew about two houses and their families the 'Bakers' who were bakers in the village and the Lewises. Bob asked me and I was able to tell him I knew of the two houses, 'Swiss

Cottage' and "Florence Terrace', also Edwin baker (the baker) and his family as the last Baker was John Edwin baker (his father was Edwin) and I went to school with two of his children in the village in the 1940s and I worked with his other two sons when I was printing. The lady's other family was the Lewises, and I have photos of her great grandfather who was the manager of Taunton Brick and Tile Company on Wellington New Road and although they came and tried to find them, they couldn't. I knew Swiss Cottage and it was pulled down when the brickyard ceased to operate in the 60s. I think it was when the brickyard closed down that we lost our Scout Hut that sat for many years just along the roundabout on the brickyard side of the New Road. This was when the scouts went over to the Trident at Galmington and the hut became just 'Firewood'.

Monday 12th March, St. Gregory

Pope Gregory the Great, patrol of scholars, died in about 604. He sent Augustine and his monks as Christian missionaries to England, where St Gregory's day used to be remembered by husbandmen who called 12th March 'Farmers Day'.

Saturday 3rd march 2012

Today is mine and my wife Margaret's 50th
Wedding anniversary. We were married at St
Peter's Church Lyngford, a new church at that
time. I bought several bricks and roofing tiles
which was a way of raising money toward the
new build. We are having a get together for
family and friends on the day. But going through
the guest list for our marriage only three guests
are still alive from then and one of these is my
niece who at the age of four was one of my
bridesmaids. We went on honeymoon to London
at the Edwardian 'Kenilworth Hotel'. We lived
high or a week. It is still there on the corner of
Great Russell Street. So that is the first 50 years
so the rest should be plain sailing.

Occasional Wafflings of a Villager
Autumn 2012

When chestnut leaves do fall
Cotton ain't no good at all.

Well here I am again, how time flies where you aren't committed. I have had an unusual time of late with bad health and my wife having a heart bypass operation. In the light of this I reluctantly resigned from being secretary of the Bishop's Hull flower show. I was afraid it would stop, but it was kept going by Val and Clem Pryer and a very good job they made of it, so I can sleep well now.

The show was a great success and as I told many at the show, I can now have all the pleasure with none of the pain. I would like to take this opportunity to thank not only the committee who have helped me over the many year, but some of the village stalwarts who have given of their time and energies without having to be asked. Names that spring to mind like Kenny Guppy, Gordon Hooper, Jill Trenchard, Stella Batten, Pat Richards, John Rigby and so on. What sterling work they have performed over the years.

A good October and a good blast
To blow the hog, acorn and mast.

What a growing season we have had, drought, floods, high winds etc. all giving the grower problems with crops. Slugs, snails, because of the warm wet weather have been arriving in their droves. I netted my espalier cherry tree against the blackbirds but found snails eating them just before ripening so I only picked a dozen instead of the 5 – 6 lbs. I have enjoyed strawberries but they needed more sun, raspberries, loganberries and at the present some lovely blackberries (Loch Ness). Too early yet for my top fruit like apples and pears although I have had some plums.

Tomatoes have done well considering the lack of sun and I have picked red, pink, orange, green and black varieties which makes a beautiful salad with home grown basil and feta cheese. I have just taken a good crop of my named geranium cuttings, 56 in also there is some potting up to be done soon. I was disappointed with my broad beans as they cropped on and off because lack of sun meant lack of bees, just when they started flowering. My runner beans on the other hand have performed well and I have squirreled away 4 and a half pounds in salt for a rainy day as I am not a lover of frozen beans.

I grew some Spanish 'Padron' peppers this year which is said to have one in twelve which is super hot; well I tried some fried in olive oil as a tapas and the first one was quite nice with a very little heat, the second just blew my mouth into orbit. It was so hot and I can normally take chillies ok.

Now that it is October
Don they woolly smock

I have been busy making smoked bacon, faggots, and sausages, you have to keep your hand in and I usually give my daughter and family some as they love home produced food. My daughter often makes smoked bacon too and bread and butter. I haven't made any cheese for a while so I must have a go again as it is a beautiful strong Cheddar type that goes down well with homemade chutney or piccalilli.

Now I have some of this years 'fuggles' hops I will make some of my beer for Christmas, just a couple of gallons. This is as good as you would pay £3.00 a pint for and cost me only £1.20 per gallon to make. As said I grow my own fuggles hops and with crystal malt and two jars of mal extract makes a beautiful bitter ('Bishops Ale') much loved by my son and son-in-law.

Talking of Christmas now is a good time to make chutneys, piccalillis, pickled onions, red cabbage, pickled cauliflower, pears, eggs, etc. etc. for the Christmas period. I am whilst the tomatoes are still producing well, making tomato toppings for pizzas and tomato sauces for pasta dishes and all can be frozen to give a little taste of summer in the long dark winter days. Now my gardening days are not as productive we have a fruit and veg box weekly and also a lady in the lane has hens so we buy her eggs weekly and very fresh they are too. When you have them laid that day, you realize what a difference it makes to have them fresh.

Whilst on a rant about food it is worth mentioning that October is the start of the game season so rabbits, pheasants, partridges, wild duck, hare, pigeon, snipe, woodcock, venison are all available and our butcher Tim usually gets rabbits, pheasants, venison, so do give them a go, I am sure you will like them. The other day I found some tea (small wild ducks) in my freezer that a friend had given me and what a fine dinner they made stuffed with sage and onion with some of my runner beans and roast potatoes. It was truly one of those meals you could have eaten all over again. I have just had some 'Longhorn' beef from Sheppys and it had a taste of the past, truly beautiful. When I was a boy nearly all beef cattle were longhorn not like today with Charolais and Simmental crosses.

If the hare wears a thick coat in October, then lay in a good stock of fuel.

I was thinking the other day of how the village has changed since I was a boy. We then knew everyone in the village but now there are the new estates behind Bishop's Hull Road, new one on the Silk Mills road, all the development that is Heron Drive, and the side roads, Walnut Close, Badgers Green, Jarmyns, Bakers Close and all the other side roads and closes, off Westfield Drive, Gillards, Farrant Close, Shutewater Close,

then Malthouse Court, Parsonage, Haydon Close
and several houses that were built behind
Magnolia House which was called
'Greensleeves' I think. So as you see a lot of
building – "where next" I wonder.
My bungalow was built in Mountway Lane
whilst I was growing up in the early 50s. There
are more coming to me like Richmond Park
behind Mountway Lane and more houses built by
the T.A. on Mountway Road. If you know of any
more forgive me for my memory ain't what it
was. I always close with a recipe so here goes.
Cheap and cheerful.

Corned Beef Hash

8 oz corned beef
4 oz butterbeans or haricot beans soaked
overnight (or tinned)
2 dessertspoons pear barley
1 beef stock cube, crushed
2 onions chopped
1 carrot thinly sliced
2 oz turnip or swede finely diced
1 bay leaf
salt and pepper to taste

If using dried beans put them in a pan with all
the other ingredients except the corned beef,
cover with boiling stock and oil slowly until the
beans are cooked, stirring occasionally. Then add
the beef cut into little cubes and thicken the hash

with a little flour. If you use tinned beans add at this point. Heat through and serve with a mix of potato, swede and carrot mash.

Enjoy.

Occasional Wafflings of a Villager, Christmas 2012

I wish you all a happy, healthy and peaceful Christmas and New Year.

At Christmas play and make good cheer,
For Christmas comes by once a year.

Well here we are at my favourite time of year next to spring, ie Christmas time. I have always loved it, not for presents as that is and always was the last thing on my mind. I just love the people's change in attitude generally, they are more tolerant and generally more pleasurable. I think it's the getting together of families and sharing time and pleasantries that make people more amenable at this time. We love to do things for others and share our special Christmas food and it is always appreciated so we feel good.
I am a great one for traditions and I even like my cards to be traditional, snow scenes with coaches and horses, churches covered in snow and so on. I don't like little teddy bears with ribbons and puppies etc. I think its called being very old fashioned but again, I do live in the past a bit. My feelings are, the best way forward is to go back. I remember Christmas parties in the village firstly at the old school with the gas lights on (the only ones there were), and our governors Sir Geoffrey Farrant and Miss Lythal from Barr house. The party was simple but very well done and all went

home happy. I was invited on Boxing day with my friend to the Merson family next to the Baker's shop. Mr Merson used to ring with his family, the church bells, he also umpired the village cricket team. Well, we used to play cards for matchsticks and I often lost boxes of them, but we had tea and then it was time for home. I also remember at my first school I started at the ripe old age of three, St John's off Castle Street. The war was just finishing and coming up to our Christmas party we were asked to bring to school 2oz margarine and 2 oz sugar each to make the Christmas cake. The parties there were more well done as we had marionettes, a religious tableau, a choir and Father Saunders and father Jennings led us into carols. I love my Christmas dinner, and we all know where to get a superb turkey from and I have never had a poor one in all the years I've been back.

St. Thomas grey, St. Thomas grey,
The longest night and the shortest day.

December has many of my favourite foods in season like partridge, pheasant, rabbit, wild duck, hare, woodcock and so on. There is so much taste and flavour compared to most meats today. I am convinced it's the way our meats are reared and treated. Beef was grown in the fields eating fresh grasses and herbs but now most often in sheds with hay, straw and silage to feed from.

Pigs too were kept outdoors but again most often now in sheds, pens, etc. I can look back to when I was a boy and a neighbour of ours kept pigs in the lane behind the 'Trident'. I used to go around the houses picking up potato rinds and kitchen waste in an old pram and we would boil it in an old copper boiler with a fire under it and then add barley meal to it and feed the pigs. It was known as swill and the pigs loved it. His pork tasted great.

My father and a mate kept a couple of pigs during and just after the war in the grounds of the old gas works which was managed by Mr Harris of the Manor House Bishop's Hull. It was where he got his nickname 'gassy Harris'. He, and my father would walk home from the gas works occasionally with a half pig over his shoulder and it was then that mother started making bacon, brawn, and salted down some of the pork as we had no fridges in those days. We lived like lords when we had a half pig to eat.

Looking back we used to live quite well when I was a lad and as said, we had occasional pork, we always had chickens, ducks, and at Christmas we had two geese. We also had plenty of eggs, both chicken and duck. We grew lots of vegetables so there was always plenty of food on the table. Mother was a good cook and everything was made from scratch. Father used to say, "she could make something out of nothing and even a good soup using the bones from her stays".

In the summer because of no refrigeration milk often went "on the turn" so mother used to make a soft cheese a bit like cottage cheese and it was good with home made rolls and pickles. We always had plenty of rabbits and they could be bought from a neighbour for 6d. old money and we as kids got 3d. back on the skins. We also had trout and eels as a treat and they were so nice, but today eels are not so plentiful which is a great pity. I remember when I was an apprentice printer, we had our own skittles team and a mate and I used to go out fishing for eels and I would jelly them and take a large sweet jar full to the match to eat and they were always knocked back with relish.

Blessed be St. Stephen, there's no fasting upon his evem.

There is so much food in season now, despite the winter weather. All the game is out there to be had and what a change from the general meats. We have partridges one of my favourites and also wild duck ie mallard. I do like pigeons too and the breast fried very rare is indeed a treat. My wife went to Salisbury in September and while looking around the farmers market spotted some grouse. Well, she had to buy me one as she is very aware of my likes and it was divine. I stuffed it with sage and onion put a little bacon on the top to stop it drying out and roasted it with some game chips and runner beans; I was in heaven.

I also bought at Rumwell farm shop, a brace of partridge and a wild mallard duck. I am always OK for fruit and now have 20 fruit trees in my small garden, apples, pears, plums, cherries, figs, not to mention three grapes, raspberries, blackberries, loganberries, strawberries and rhubarb. I have had despite the season, lots of tomatoes so have made pizza toppings for the freezer.

I have started talking of food again so I will go straight to me recipe which is a Christmas Day vegetarian alternative.

A Vegetarian Christmas Pie

3 oz lentils rinsed
7 oz portabello mushrooms finely chopped
1 teasp. Veg bouillon powder
2 teasp. Dried mixed herbs
1 tbspn sunflower oil
3 oz chopped mixed nuts
2 large leeks sliced
3 oz pitted prunes, chopped
2 cloves garlic chopped
1 oz fresh breadcrumbs
2 eggs beaten
salt and black pepper
2 sheets ready rolled puff pastry 15 oz
flour for dusting

Pre-heat oven 220C, gas 7

Put the lentils in a pan with the veg stock and
water to cover, simmer until tender. Set aside.
In a frying pan add oil, leeks and garlic,
mushrooms and herbs and cook until tender.
Transfer to a bowl and add nuts, prunes, lentils
and breadcrumbs.
Add 2./3rds of the beaten egg to mixture and
season, put aside to cool.
Take one sheet of pastry and dampen the edges,
lay on baking sheet. Spoon the mixture over the
pastry base keeping away from the edges.
Lay the other sheet on top and squeeze the edges
together, seal and crimp. Cut the top pastry about

1/2 an inch apart for effect when risen. Brush the top with egg wash and bake for 25 – 30 minutes until golden brown.
 Serve hot.

I am having a turkey or goose.

Enjoy, Roy Baker

Occasional Wafflings of a Villager,
Spring (March) 2013

The spring has sprung the grass has ris
I wonder where the birdie is,
The bird is on the wing, but that's absurd,
The wing is on the bird.

Spring is here and what a lovely time we should
have now with new leaves on the trees, shrubs,
etc. Daffodils flowering and spreading their
golden hues and making people cheery after the
long wet winter months. Next month we will be
looking for St. George's mushrooms and the
expensive morels. Now we can start growing our
vegetables for the new season. What a great start
for the new season. I am already under way with
cabbage, Tuscan black kale, Brussels sprouts,
lettuce, broad beans, beetroot all in the
greenhouse in trays and ready to plant out soon.
Early tomatoes are potted on and outdoor ones
sown together with courgettes, cucumbers,
pepper and chillies.

I had had to buy some new seeds of a few of my
favourite tomatoes as I have had the seed for
many years (at least 20 years) and they go down
hill and cross pollinate so you get a tom while
although good, it's not the pure type you require.
I have found them after a long hunt, at 'Nicky's
seeds' online.

I do love my tomatoes and at the last week of
January I ate my last fresh one so back to frozen

tomato products until mid June when we pick again.

There is still time to do your very last fruit tree pruning and roses. Last year I grew old varieties of runner bean, 'Scarlet Emperor' and 'Kelvedon Masterpiece' and I knew as soon as I tasted it, I'd found the old runner bean taste that I had been missing for years, so I will certainly grow Scarlet Emperor again this year with 'White Lady' which is another good one.

Through January and February I have had some good lettuce outside with no protection and have cut some good heads, the variety was 'Webb's Wonderful' and with my tomatoes still with me together with some beetroots made a good salad. I took some cuttings from my chrysanthemums as they did very well last year. I rooted them in a heated propagator which only takes about two weeks then they can be potted on. I have ended up with 39 nice geranium plants which have been potted and are growing apace and flowering. They are mainly for planters and baskets outdoors. I must sow some lobelia to enhance them, usually 'Trailing Sapphire'.

Upon St. David's day put oats and barley in the clay.

As I write this we have between us made another batch of brown sauce, I never buy 'Daddies' any more as it isn't so good in my estimation. I have been putting away a selection of game for the 'off' season which is the end of January for partridge and wild mallard duck, and the end of February for pheasants. Rabbits can be had even out of season if necessary but I like to have them before March as young ones are around then. My mate goes up to Leicester shooting on a mutual friend's farm and he passes on to me some venison, usually roe deer but also fallow and muntjac deer. I have had also partridges, pheasants and a hare, all lovely meats which are like super foods as there is no fat with them. Muntjac deer has no closed season so they can be taken at anytime. I really think that rabbits are still a very good food and it is a pity that people after all this time still go on about myxomatosis and although it can still be seen around at times it is not the terrible killer it once was, and the humble rabbit still takes some beating for taste and flavour, and I for one wouldn't be without one. I have been eating them since a child and I have eaten them with the tell tale marks of myxy on them and I am still here to tell the tale, although I can't remember hopping around quite so much as I do lately.

A wet March makes a sad harvest.

I am a great fan of fish and thankfully now even the supermarkets are flying the flag to invite us to use more sustainable types and I am all for it. I regularly buy Pollack, pouting, whiting, huss, dabs, flounder, megrim, sprats, mackerel, herrings, whitebait, black bream, conger, even coley, etc and they are lovely, often far more flavourful than cod or haddock and are less expensive. A piece of skate (ray) poached with black pepper and capers is a dish well worth waiting for.

I am too in search of a regular supplier of mutton, how we have left that back in the past I do not know. I well remember as a lad, mother boiling a leg of mutton and serving it with a caper sauce and spring greens, how good that was. There are many foods like that which to my mind should be resurrected and brought back to the present. There are foods out there which I still do use that are almost forgotten and yet they can be beautiful like oxtail, ox cheeks, hearts, lamb, pig and ox, beautifully stuffed and roasted, sweetbreads, trotters, melts, tongues and so on, most are less expensive and they may remind you of your youth during the war.

March search, April try, May will prove whether you live or die.

I used to help a chap who lived not far from us who kept pigs. We often went back to his house where he would say "come on boy, I am feeling peckish". He was an ex Japanese prisoner of war and he would say "sit down at the table boy" and he would slice onions, roughly chop corned beef, fry them in a pan and add an amount of curry powder. As a child this went down well and believe it or not to this day I recreate that dish with a few modifications and still enjoy it, and when I make it he is in my mind.

On Mothering Sunday above all other
Every Child should dine with its Mother.

I have after all these years found a seed merchant that provides many types of vegetable seeds and also many varieties of each type. I have found some of my old varieties of tomato which although I have saved seeds for at least twenty years these are now declining and are cross pollinating so now I have received new stock of tomato, Pink Brandywine, Yellow Brandywine, Black Ananas (pineapple) and also a mix of heritage varieties. The seeds man is 'Nicky's seeds' these are online so do have a look. I can verify that they are very swift and reliable. For many years I bought my seeds from Edwin Tucker of Devon but all my old varieties seem to have been dropped in favour of a new continental breeder and all seeds are prefixed with RZ known as Rijk Zwaan. I am not happy with this.

I was thinking the other day that when I was a lad all local mums together with their children would gather and do on a mass walk to the copse near West Buckland. We would pick primroses and tie bunches on a small hazel stick to bring home. They would take sandwiches (usually egg or marmite) and bottles of homemade lemonade. It was a fantastic time we all had and yet how simple, everyone got on well and we shared what we had including prams and pushchairs if it got too much for little legs. I don't see anything like this happening today and yet it would do the youngsters of today the world of good to get away from their computer games, etc, and interact with their neighbours.

As a boy I would go out fishing over Roughmoor and catch eels and an occasional brown trout or perch, I would take them home so proud that I was putting something on the table. Boys did that in those days. I would climb a tree to get pigeon eggs and on the river banks to get moorhen eggs and we ate them honey sweet. I would go into the fields at 18 acres and pick wild field mushrooms and I could never get enough as I loved the black gravy that they produced in the cooking.

All this talk of trout and wild mushrooms has got me to thinking of my recipe for the month and as it is spring what about:

Skate with black butter and capers, for two

2 pieces of skate wing
1 small onion
1 bay leaf
2 oz butter
2 tbsp. Cider vinegar or white wine vinegar
1 tbsp chopped parsley
salt to taste.

Put skate into pan, side by side, not on top of each another. Add sliced onion, salt, bay leaf and boiling water. Heat until boiling then simmer gently for 10 minutes until flesh parts from the bones.

Lift skate out of pan and on to warm plate, cover and keep warm.

Now to cook the sauce, melt butter in a pan, cook gently until it turns golden brown. Drizzle over fish.

Add vinegar to the hot pan and allow it to bubble gently until slightly reduced. Drizzle this over the fish.

Scatter the capers and parsley in the pan to just warm and scatter over the fish and serve immediately.

Serve with boiled small Jersey Royals and steamed purple sprouting spears.

Enjoy, Roy Baker

Occasional Wafflings of a Villager
June 2013

A swarm of bees in June is worth a silver spoon.

Here we are 'Summer', I wonder how wet this year will be. I have plenty of tomatoes, cucumbers, peppers chillies, courgettes, etc to see me through summer, autumn and early winter. My runner beans that did so well last year I decided to change varieties; firstly a new slant on an old variety which has bags of taste from Scarlet Emperor has now been revamped as Scarlet Empire; it is said to have the old true bean taste with improved growing etc. I am also growing White Lady which is again and foolproof variety of good taste. I am also growing a few early ones called Lady Di, along with Kelvedon masterpiece, and Scarlet Emperor. So a total of five varieties in all.

My broad beans have been very good, it's an old variety a couple of us have kept going since the 1960s and has long been out of production, Dobies Rentpayer. This year, because of the very bad weather, floods, etc., long developing greens that have been underwater have succumbed to rot but in my garden I have had some outstanding purple sprouting broccoli and have noticed in the farm shops it was £7.99 per kilo and that's just because it has been so hard to get any at all.

Kales have been, although said to be the hardiest vegetable, hard to get hold of and most of ours

came from Spain. I am more and more
determined to obtain my food from local sources.
Because I can't grow so much veg these days I
have a vegetable box delivered from a local lad
including free range eggs, aracuna and cream
legbars which are green and blue. The eggs are
thick and creamy and very orange in the yolk and
that is well worth the money and tastes great.
 I must say I love Sheppys Longhorn beef, we
have had shin, rump steaks, sirloin steaks, brisket
and it has all been very tasty, and you can see the
cattle from the Wellington Road so they are very
local.

Calm weather in June, sets all in tune.

 June is the month when I think of cooking
outdoors and sharing food. I like my bar-b-que;
it's an old brick thing I knocked up but is brilliant
for cooking. I always use lumpwood charcoal and
once you get it going, it seems to go on forever. I
also have a chimnea made of cast iron and it is
brilliant for cooking whole joints etc on wood
fire, so you get some of the smoky taste in your
food. I sometimes combine my little hot smoker,
as well as smoked trout, mackerel, and chicken;
it's a nice change.
 I once remember Fred Yeandle brought me up a
nice sized trout and I smoked it and made some
smoked trout pate. I took some down to Fred and,
on the Monday, he said to me laughingly, "Don't
bring any more of that pate down as Jo had me

making toast all weekend." Fred was something else, wasn't he?

I remember when he put a recipe in the church cook book edited and produced by Mai Curnow. His recipe was for a trout pie, but he finished the recipe with the words, "If you are unable to catch your trout see Fred anytime between March and October". I don't know how many trout that comment cost him but he meant it.

Another well-known and lovely lady I think of often was my neighbour May Day. What a lovely lady she was, always thinking and doing for others. People would pop in and see her, often for her advice or wisdom. I often went in with a bowl of Stilton and celery soup and a hand made roll which was her favourite and she always appreciated it. I would be in chatting for an hour or even two.

I remember when she came to the village in the early 70s with her husband, Walt. They joined the Flower Show committee and were members and treasurer until around 2002 when Bob Coombs took over from her. May was a founder member of the good companions with Aunty Mary Drew, and opened her garden for teas etc. once a year in the name of The Good Companions. I was invited with the family to May's 90th birthday which I considered an honour.

Aunty Mary Drew was also a lovely lady and when she died May gave me her cookery book with all her well-known cakes etc in. I knew her since a boy of 7 years, she was in fact our dinner lady at school in Gyspy Lane, and she always managed to serve me cabbage without the pile of thick stumps, along with Mrs King of Smithy and Mrs Stark of Galmington and late of the Malthouse.

24th St. John or Midsummer day.
cut your thistles before St John, you will have
two instead of one.

I love sourdough bread and to this end I have started another batch of sourdough starter (no added yeast), this takes ay least a week to develop before you can use it to make bread. I have always looked at bakers making sourdough bread and they do the second proving in a round 'Banneton' handmade basket which leaves the telltale rope marks around the loaf. I brought the baskets from eBay and didn't realize they came directly from Shanghai through China post and took a few weeks to arrive here. Well when I make some loaves they should look perfect.

I will now start my recipe, I found this one in an old cook book and it's local, so here goes.

TAUNTON TEMPTATION

1 lb boneless pork
1 oz seasoned flour
1 tablespoon cooking oil
1 large onion sliced
2 large cooking apples, peeled, cored and sliced
1 teaspoon mixed herbs
salt and pepper
1/2 pint medium cider
1 1/2 lbs potatoes peeled and thinly sliced
1 oz butter, melted

Toss pork into seasoned flour and fry in the oil until brown and put into the casserole.
Fry the onion for 5 minutes, add apples, herbs, salt and pepper and cider, bring to the boil then pour over pork in the casserole.
Arrange slices of potato on top, overlapping, and brush with melted butter, cover and cook 180oC gas mark 4 for 1 1/4 hours.
Remove foil lid, increase heat to 220oC gas mark 7 and continue cooking for a further 15 minutes until brown.

As broad beans and asparagus are in season serve these with the meal.

Enjoy.
Roy Baker.